MAD for MATH

MAKE SPACE FOR GEOMETRY

THIS BOOK IS FOR CHILDREN AGED 8-10

EDITED BY MATTIA CRIVELLINI

ILLUSTRATIONS BY AGNESE BARUZZI

LET'S START DOING... GEOMETRY IN SPACE!

"Mathematics expresses values that reflect the cosmos, including orderliness, balance, harmony, logic, and abstract beauty."
—*Deepak Chopra*

Math is a useful and tangible universal language that is always present around us. Geometry, in particular, immersed as it is in shapes and space, helps the child to learn new concepts and to apply them to their everyday experiences.
The imaginative narrative you'll find in these pages allows children's minds to wander into new worlds, increasing their personal involvement in the problems presented and sparking their imagination.
The three actions underpinning each challenge are reading, observing, and understanding. Have fun!

CONTENTS
- Basic elements of plane geometry: points, lines, angles
- Polygons
- Solid figures
- Isometries
- How to calculate area
- Problem-solving games
- Lateral thinking games

FOR CHILDREN AGED 8-10

SOME TIPS FOR ADULTS

Respect children when they need time and when they "refuse" something!
If they close the book or skip a page it doesn't mean they are throwing in the towel; they may just need a little time to think about the topics calmly.

Ask questions, don't give answers!
If the child asks you for help, do not give them the answer.
Use targeted questions instead to help them focus on the problem or mistake.

Let children find their own way, even if it is long and winding!
Later, you can guide them to explore other routes and maybe discover more "clever" ways of getting to the solution.

The first step to solving is understanding
Help children rework the proposed situations, by verbalizing, drawing, or using concrete materials, before searching for a solution or performing a calculation.
That is the easiest part of the job!

Ask "how did you do that?"
Get them accustomed little by little to explaining their reasoning.
It is much more important to know how and why they came up with the answer than to know the name of the rule applied.

The situations presented in the book are fictitious by nature.
Help children track down numbers and math in everyday life.
Step out of the book and get to know the math!

LOOK AT THE STARS!

>32JJ PH 3PK<6N/ ?09| Z=@ 19PP8P@ =A G9C<>@ M/ PN :2U3
2G/| Z3 =Z7:J1 ?J76 ZO P>B"+ VP2}#TU PH+PK ? @ D 14C3 2H?
... TRANSLATOR ACTIVATED!

> HI! LET ME INTRODUCE MYSELF.
> I AM A SPACE EXPLORER. MY NAME IS CX10-742Y,
> BUT YOU, YOUNG EARTHLING, CAN CALL ME CYX.

As an explorer, my task is to deepen our knowledge of the universe. A journey to a fantastic world awaits us, one with completely different rules from those we are used to. First, however, we must read a manual called "Basic Training for Space Explorers in the Field of Geometry."

You should know that when you travel very far, one of the things that changes is the sky under which we sleep. Just as on Earth, different stars are visible in the sky depending on the southern or northern hemisphere of the planet from which we observe them. Ready? The time has come to look at the constellations from a different point of view—an explorer's look at the geometric universe!

HERE ARE SOME EXAMPLES OF **TERRESTRIAL CONSTELLATIONS**.

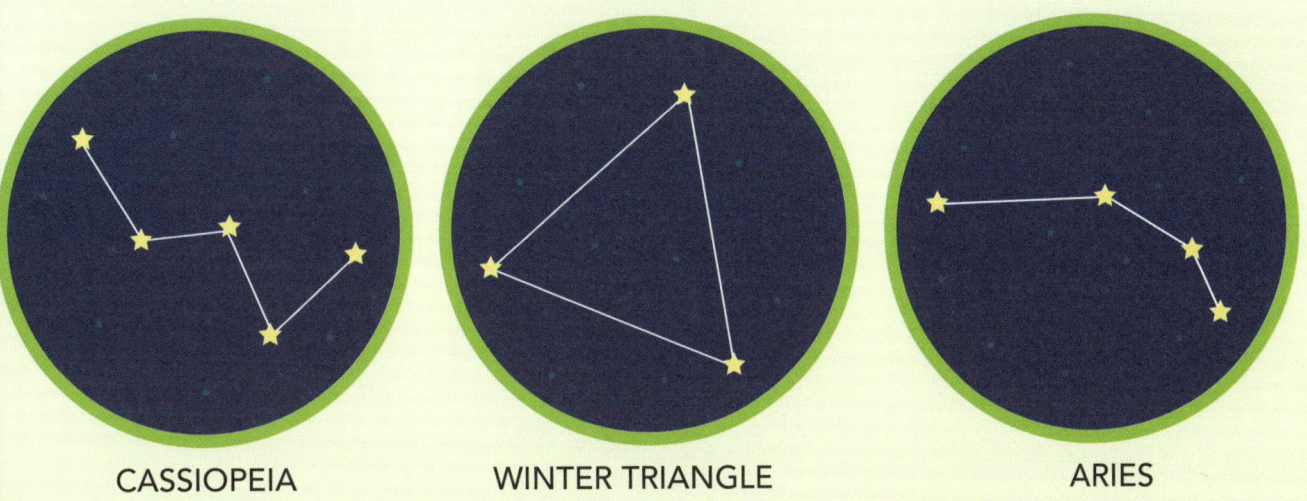

CASSIOPEIA   WINTER TRIANGLE   ARIES

IF YOU LOOK AT THEM CAREFULLY, THE CONSTELLATIONS APPEAR AS DIFFERENT COMBINATIONS OF LINES.

- WE CALL A LINE CONSISTING OF SEVERAL SEGMENTS **BROKEN**.

- WE CALL A LINE IN WHICH THE FIRST AND LAST VERTEX CONNECT **BROKEN CLOSED**.

- WE CALL A LINE IN WHICH THE FIRST AND LAST VERTEX DO NOT CONNECT **BROKEN OPEN**.

- IF IN A BROKEN LINE TWO SIDES OVERLAP, WE CALL THE BROKEN LINE **CROSSED**.

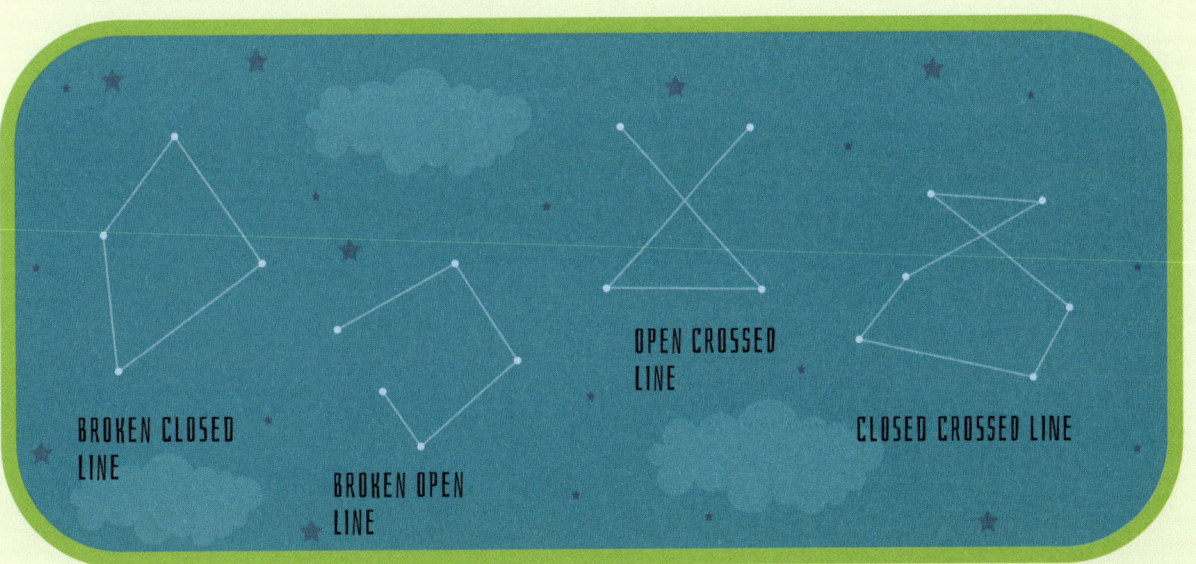

BROKEN CLOSED LINE

BROKEN OPEN LINE

OPEN CROSSED LINE

CLOSED CROSSED LINE

SO, YOUNG ASSISTANT, YOU JUST HAVE TO GO OUT… AND LOOK AT THE STARS!

LET'S PRACTICE A LITTLE!

HERE ARE SOME OTHER CONSTELLATIONS TO IDENTIFY. CAN YOU TELL IF THE LINE IS BROKEN CLOSED, BROKEN OPEN, OPEN CROSSED, OR CLOSED CROSSED?

WRITE THE ANSWERS ON THE DOTTED LINES.

STAR ANGLES

WELCOME TO THE SECOND LESSON! WE ARE ABOUT TO DISCOVER ANOTHER IMPORTANT FEATURE OF OUR CONSTELLATIONS: **THEIR CORNERS OR ANGLES**!

WHEN BOTH PARTS OF A PLANE DIVIDED BY TWO LINES HAVE A COMMON ENDPOINT, WE CALL IT AN ANGLE.

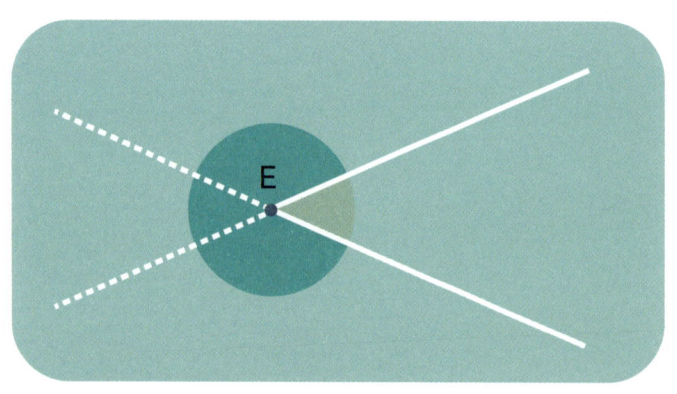

LET'S APPLY THIS INFORMATION TO OUR SKY.
ANGLES ARE NOT ALL THE SAME, AND THEY HAVE DIFFERENT NAMES TOO.
A **CONCAVE ANGLE** IS THE NAME FOR AN ANGLE THAT CONTAINS THE EXTENSIONS OF ITS LINES.
A **CONVEX ANGLE** IS AN ANGLE THAT DOES NOT CONTAIN ITS LINES.

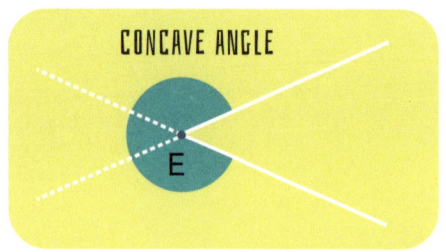 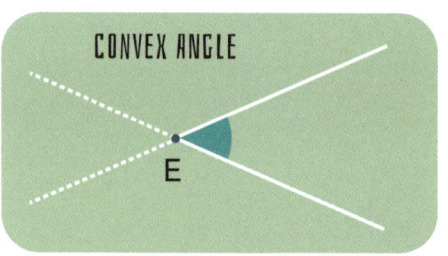

IT'S NOT OVER YET. THERE ARE OTHER SPECIAL ANGLES!
RIGHT ANGLE: HAS A WIDTH OF 90 DEGREES.
ACUTE ANGLE: HAS A WIDTH OF LESS THAN 90 DEGREES.
OBTUSE ANGLE: HAS A WIDTH GREATER THAN 90 DEGREES.

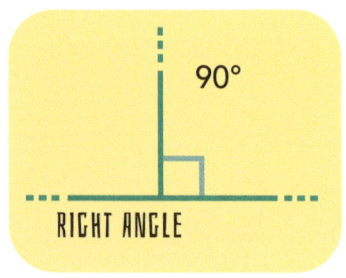 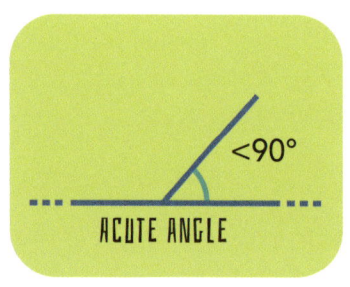 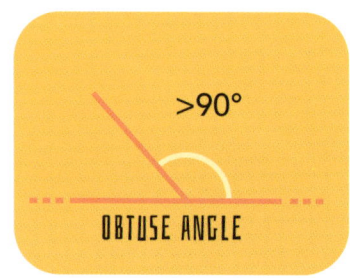

PLACE THE RIGHT, CONCAVE, AND CONVEX STICKERS ON THE FOLLOWING ANGLES:

WELCOME TO POLYGONLAND!

OUR TRAINING CONTINUES: SPACE, THE FIRST FRONTIER. WELCOME TO POLYGONLAND!

WHERE IS IT? EVERYWHERE! IT IS ALL AROUND US! MANY OBJECTS HAVE A POLYGONAL SHAPE IN OUR WORLD. TRIANGLES, QUADRILATERALS, PENTAGONS, HEXAGONS, AND PENTAGONAL STARS ARE PRESENT IN EVERYTHING THAT SURROUNDS US: FROM FLOORS TO FLAGS, FROM THE SHAPE OF BUILDINGS TO STREET SIGNS.

SO, IF YOU LEARN TO RECOGNIZE POLYGONLAND, YOU WILL REALIZE THAT IT IS ALWAYS AROUND YOU. EVEN IN THE ROOM WHERE YOU ARE NOW. YOU'LL FIND IT WHEN YOU GO OUT FOR A WALK, WHEN YOU'RE WATCHING TV, OR WHEN YOU PLAY WITH YOUR FRIENDS.

IT IS THE WORLD THAT GEOMETRY HAS PUT BEFORE YOU, TO SHOW YOU THE BEAUTY OF MATH!

HERE IS A NEW QUIZ FROM THE MANUAL.

TO SOLVE IT, LET'S FIRST LEARN HOW TO RECOGNIZE POLYGONS.
A **POLYGON** IS A CLOSED BROKEN LINE THAT IS NOT CROSSED.
REGULAR POLYGONS HAVE SIDES AND ANGLES OF THE SAME SHAPE AND SIZE.
OTHERWISE THEY ARE CALLED **IRREGULAR**.
EVERYTHING CLEAR? LET'S GIVE IT A TRY!
COLOR THE REGULAR POLYGONS GREEN AND THE IRREGULAR ONES RED.

OBSERVE THE **REGULAR** POLYGONS ON THIS PAGE.
COUNT HOW MANY SIDES AND ANGLES THEY EACH HAVE. THEN, ON THE LAST PAGES OF THE BOOK, LOOK FOR THE CORRESPONDING **IRREGULAR** POLYGON STICKERS—THAT IS, THE ONES THAT HAVE THE SAME NUMBER OF SIDES AND ANGLES—AND STICK THEM NEXT TO EACH SHAPE.

ATTACH THE IRREGULAR POLYGON STICKERS BELOW, AS SHOWN IN THE EXAMPLE:

NUMBER OF SIDES: ....
NUMBER OF ANGLES: ....

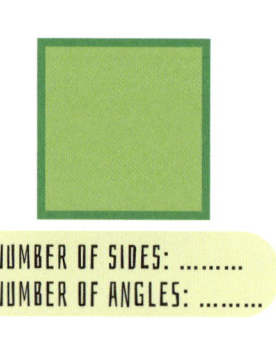

NUMBER OF SIDES: ....
NUMBER OF ANGLES: ....

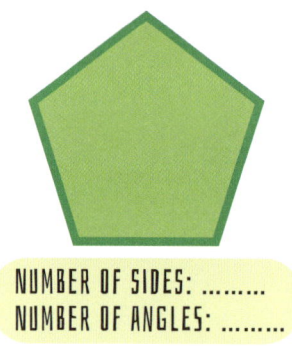

NUMBER OF SIDES: ....
NUMBER OF ANGLES: ....

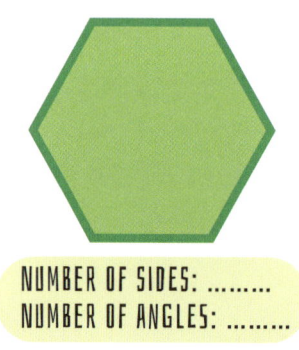

NUMBER OF SIDES: ....
NUMBER OF ANGLES: ....

NOW, LET'S CHANGE IT UP!

TAKE A LOOK AT THE **IRREGULAR** POLYGONS HERE. THEN, ON THE LAST PAGES OF THE BOOK, LOOK FOR THE CORRESPONDING **REGULAR** POLYGON STICKERS AND STICK THEM NEXT TO EACH SHAPE.

ATTACH THE REGULAR POLYGON STICKERS BELOW:

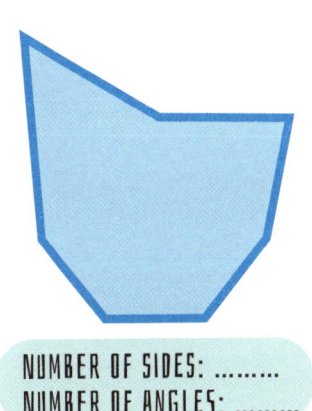

NUMBER OF SIDES: ....
NUMBER OF ANGLES: ....

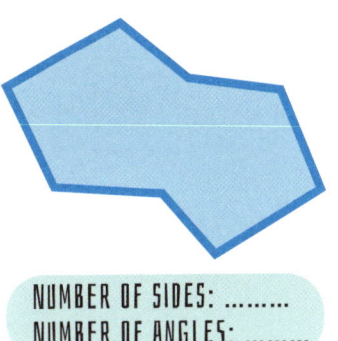

NUMBER OF SIDES: ....
NUMBER OF ANGLES: ....

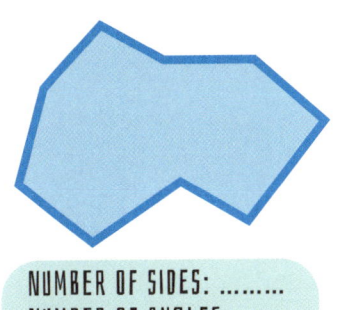

NUMBER OF SIDES: ....
NUMBER OF ANGLES: ....

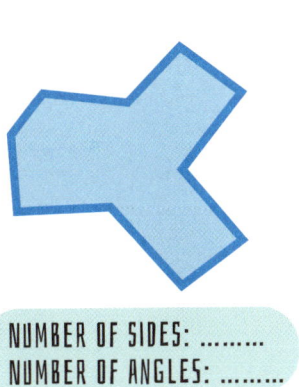

NUMBER OF SIDES: ....
NUMBER OF ANGLES: ....

TIME TO GO!

TRAINING IS COMPLETE!

It's time to visit new stars and new worlds! Here's an image of the sky visible from the star SIRIUS B. These constellations are really strange: I sent the photo to the command center and they asked me to calculate the area of each one. Hmm…I think you'll have to help me!

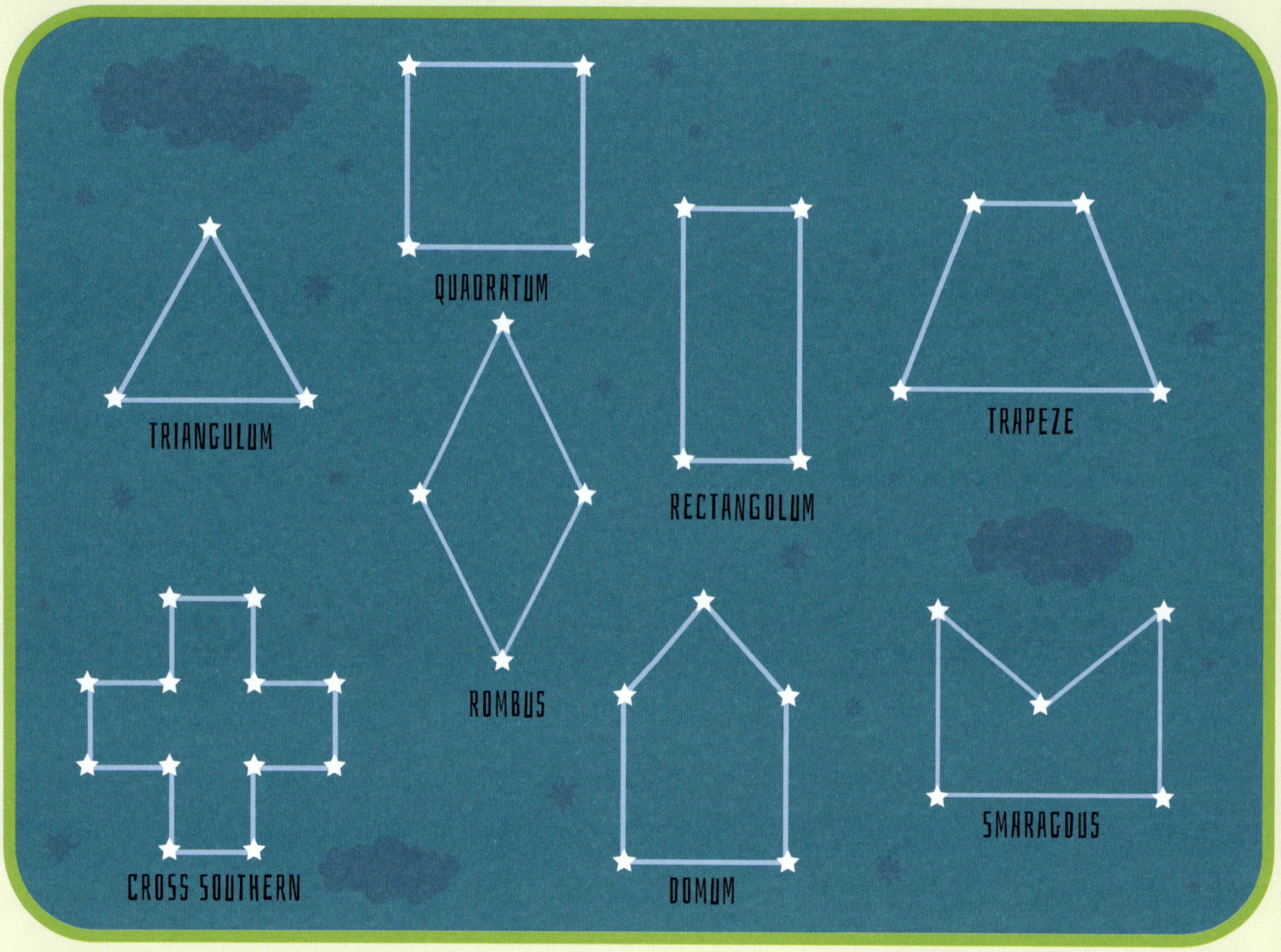

[Constellations shown: TRIANGULUM, QUADRATUM, RECTANGOLUM, TRAPEZE, ROMBUS, CROSS SOUTHERN, DOMUM, SMARAGDUS]

THIS IS THE INFORMATION THAT WE KNOW:

S = SIDE
H = HEIGHT
B = BASE

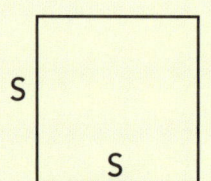

AREA OF A SQUARE = S X S

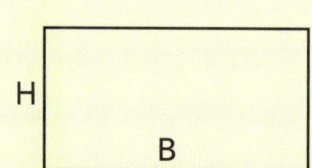

AREA OF A RECTANGLE = B X H

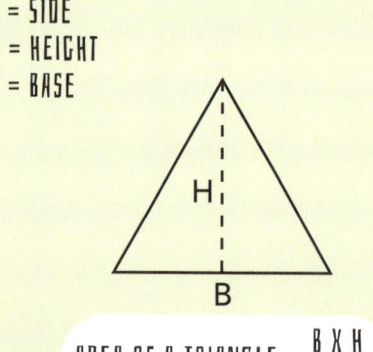

AREA OF A TRIANGLE = $\frac{B \times H}{2}$

AREA OF CONSTELLATIONS

IF YOU PLACE AN IMAGINARY SQUARE GRID OVER THE SKY OF **SIRIUS B** AND DIVIDE THE POLYGONS INTO SHAPES THAT YOU KNOW AND THAT YOU CAN CALCULATE THE AREA OF, CAN YOU COMPLETE THE MISSION? YOU SHOULD KNOW THAT EACH SIDE OF THE LITTLE SQUARES ON THE BLUE GRID MEASURES ONE INCH, AND THE AREA OF EACH LITTLE BLUE SQUARE IS ONE SQUARE INCH.

NOW CALCULATE THE AREA OF SIRIUS BOT!

DIVIDE THE POLYGON INTO SHAPES YOU KNOW AND ADD UP THEIR AREAS. CALCULATE THE AREA OF THIS ROBOT, WHO LIVES ON **SIRIUS B**.

THE GALAXIES OF LABYRINTHS

THERE ARE TWO VERY FARAWAY GALAXIES. THEY ARE CALLED **MAZE** AND **LABYRINTH**. THEY LOOK ALIKE, BUT THEY ARE ACTUALLY COMPLETELY DIFFERENT, AND ONE CANNOT BE MISTAKEN FOR THE OTHER.
LABYRINTH: A STRUCTURE WITH ONE SINGLE PATH THAT LEADS TOWARD THE CENTER. YOU CAN'T GET LOST IN THERE; YOU JUST NEED TO KEEP GOING, AND YOU'LL GET TO THE CENTER SOONER OR LATER.
MAZE: A STRUCTURE WITH DEAD ENDS, CROSSROADS, AND PERHAPS EVEN TRAPS. IT'S VERY EASY TO GET LOST.
YOU'LL FIND AN EXAMPLE OF BOTH ON THESE PAGES. FOLLOW THE PATHS AND DECIDE WHICH ONE IS THE MAZE AND WHICH ONE IS THE LABYRINTH.

THEAETETUS - THE PLATONIC SOLAR SYSTEM

WE HAVE ARRIVED AT A STRANGE SOLAR SYSTEM FORMED BY PLANETS THAT DON'T HAVE A SPHERICAL SHAPE, BUT THAT FOLLOW THE RULES OF REGULAR POLYHEDRONS—THAT IS, OBJECTS MADE FROM REGULAR POLYGONS OF THE SAME TYPE AND SIZE.

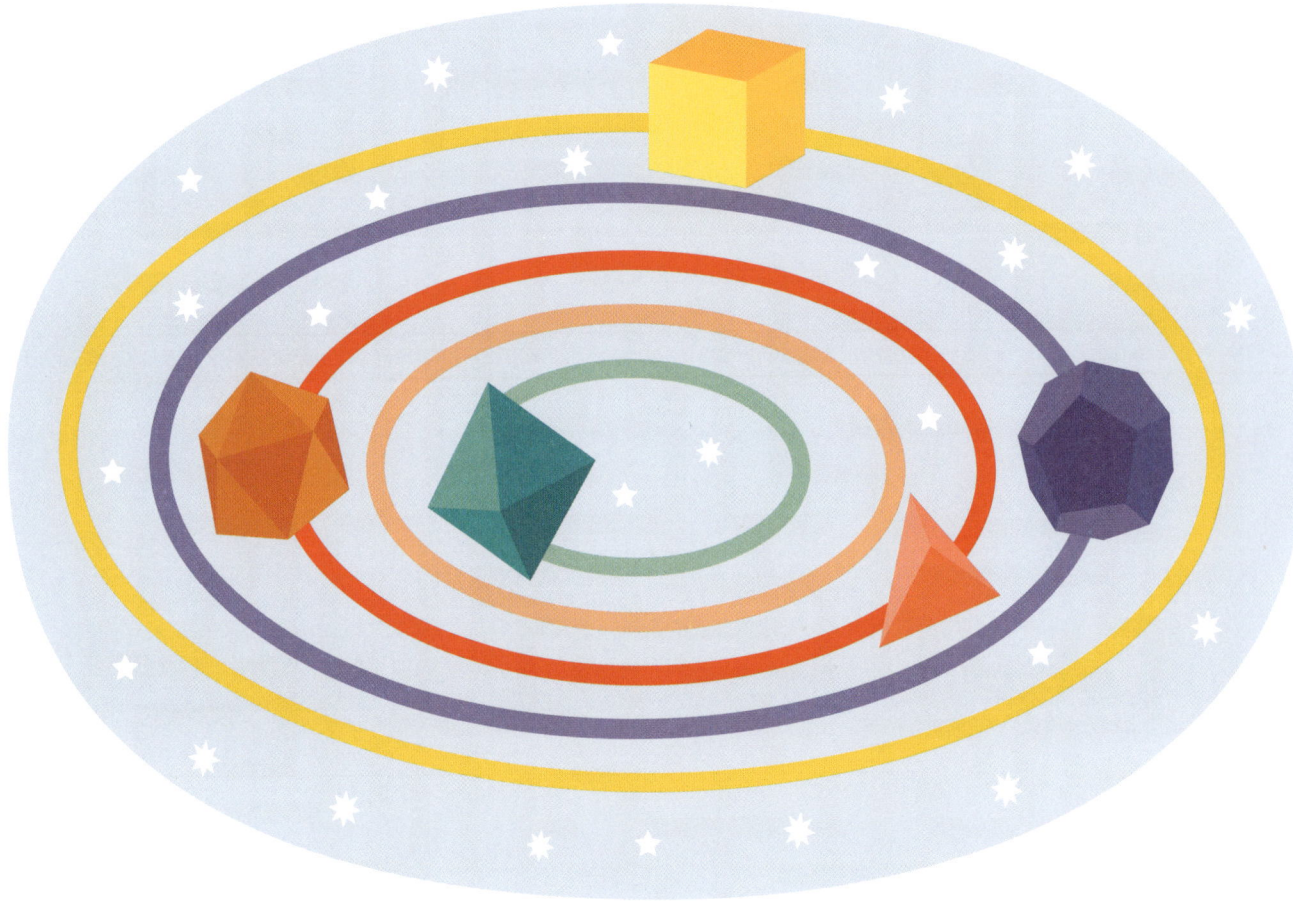

| TETRAHEDRON | CUBE | OCTAHEDRON | DODECAHEDRON | ICOSAHEDRON |

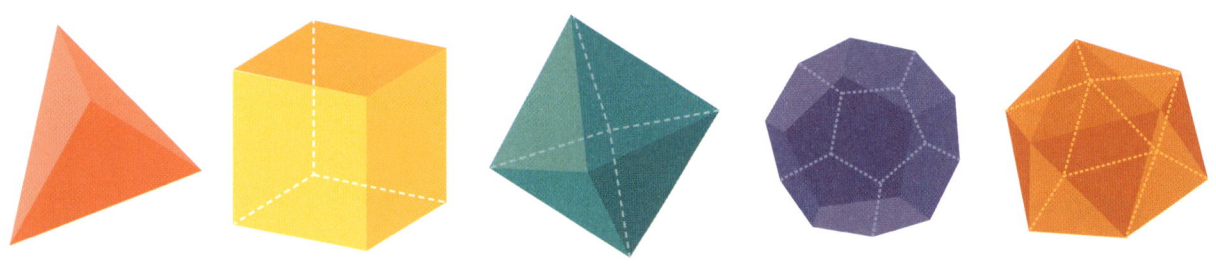

YOU CAN SEE EACH SOLID HAS FACES, EDGES, AND VERTICES.

18

EULER'S THEOREM SAYS:
THE NUMBER OF FACES MINUS THE NUMBER OF EDGES PLUS THE NUMBER OF VERTICES ALWAYS MAKES 2!

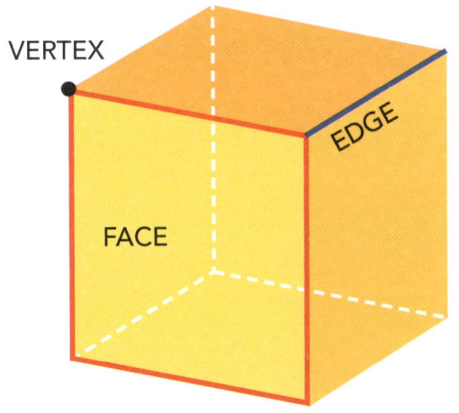

VERTEX

EDGE

FACE

EXAMPLE: CUBE

FACES=6
EDGES=12
VERTICES=8

EULER'S THEOREM F−E+V=2
6−12+8=2

TEST YOURSELF AND CALCULATE THE FIRST GEOMETRICAL SHAPES OF THEAETETUS (WE'VE GIVEN YOU HINTS): DOES EULER'S THEOREM WORK?

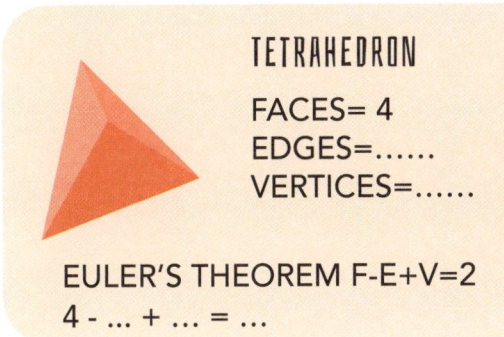

TETRAHEDRON

FACES= 4
EDGES=......
VERTICES=......

EULER'S THEOREM F-E+V=2
4 - ... + ... = ...

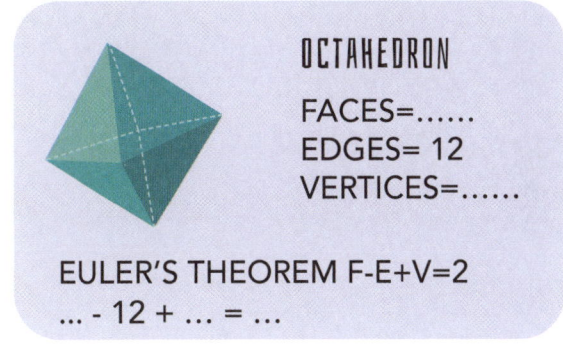

OCTAHEDRON

FACES=......
EDGES= 12
VERTICES=......

EULER'S THEOREM F-E+V=2
... - 12 + ... = ...

BE BRAVE: TEST IT OUT FOR THE DODECAHEDRON AND ICOSAHEDRON TOO.

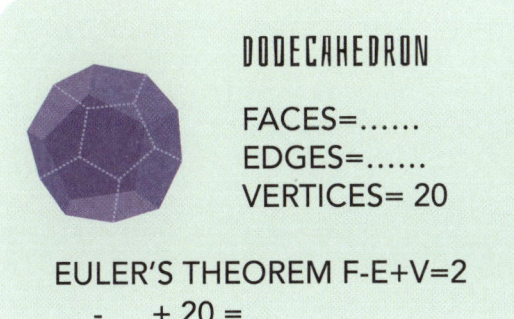

DODECAHEDRON

FACES=......
EDGES=......
VERTICES= 20

EULER'S THEOREM F-E+V=2
... - ... + 20 = ...

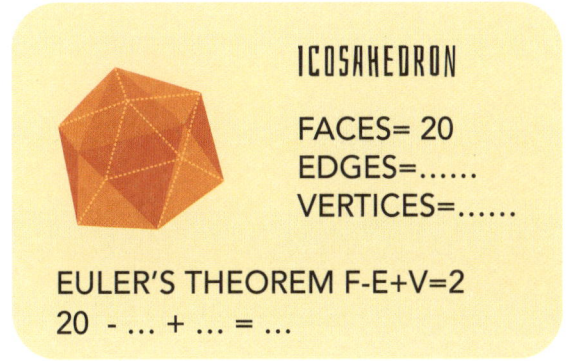

ICOSAHEDRON

FACES= 20
EDGES=......
VERTICES=......

EULER'S THEOREM F-E+V=2
20 - ... + ... = ...

HOW ARE THE PLANETS OF THE PLATONIC SOLAR SYSTEM MADE?

LET'S HAVE FUN BUILDING TWO PLATONIC PLANETS AND MAKING THEM IN THREE DIMENSIONS!

YOU WILL NEED:
1. PLATONIC SHAPES TO CUT OUT
2. SCISSORS
3. GLUE
4. STRING

STEP 1
CUT OUT THE TETRAHEDRON AND THE CUBE FROM THE FOLLOWING PAGES.

STEP 2
FOLD ALONG THE DOTTED LINES, THEN MAKE HOLES WITH A PENCIL WHERE SHOWN BY THE ARROWS.

STEP 3
TURN TO PAGE 25 AND STICK THE BASE OF THE FIGURE ONTO THE DRAWING WHERE IT SAYS "GLUE THE BASE HERE."

STEP 4
THREAD THE STRING THROUGH THE HOLES, FOLLOWING THE NUMBERS. THE ARROWS WILL HELP YOU UNDERSTAND HOW TO INSERT THE STRING.

FOLD INWARD ALONG THE DOTTED LINES.

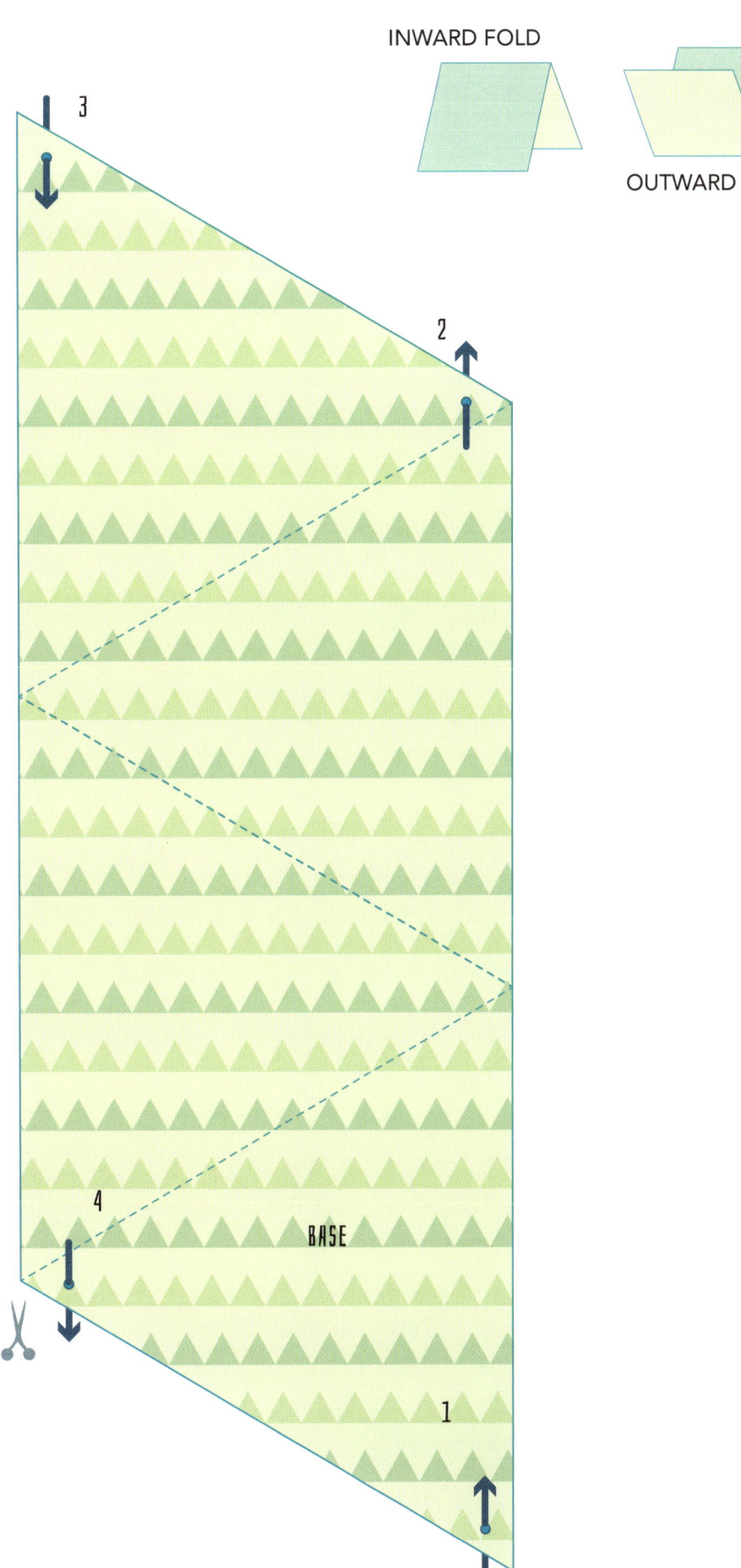

FOLLOW THE INSTRUCTIONS ON PAGE 20 TO BUILD YOUR CUBE. FOLD OUTWARD ALONG THE DOTTED LINES.

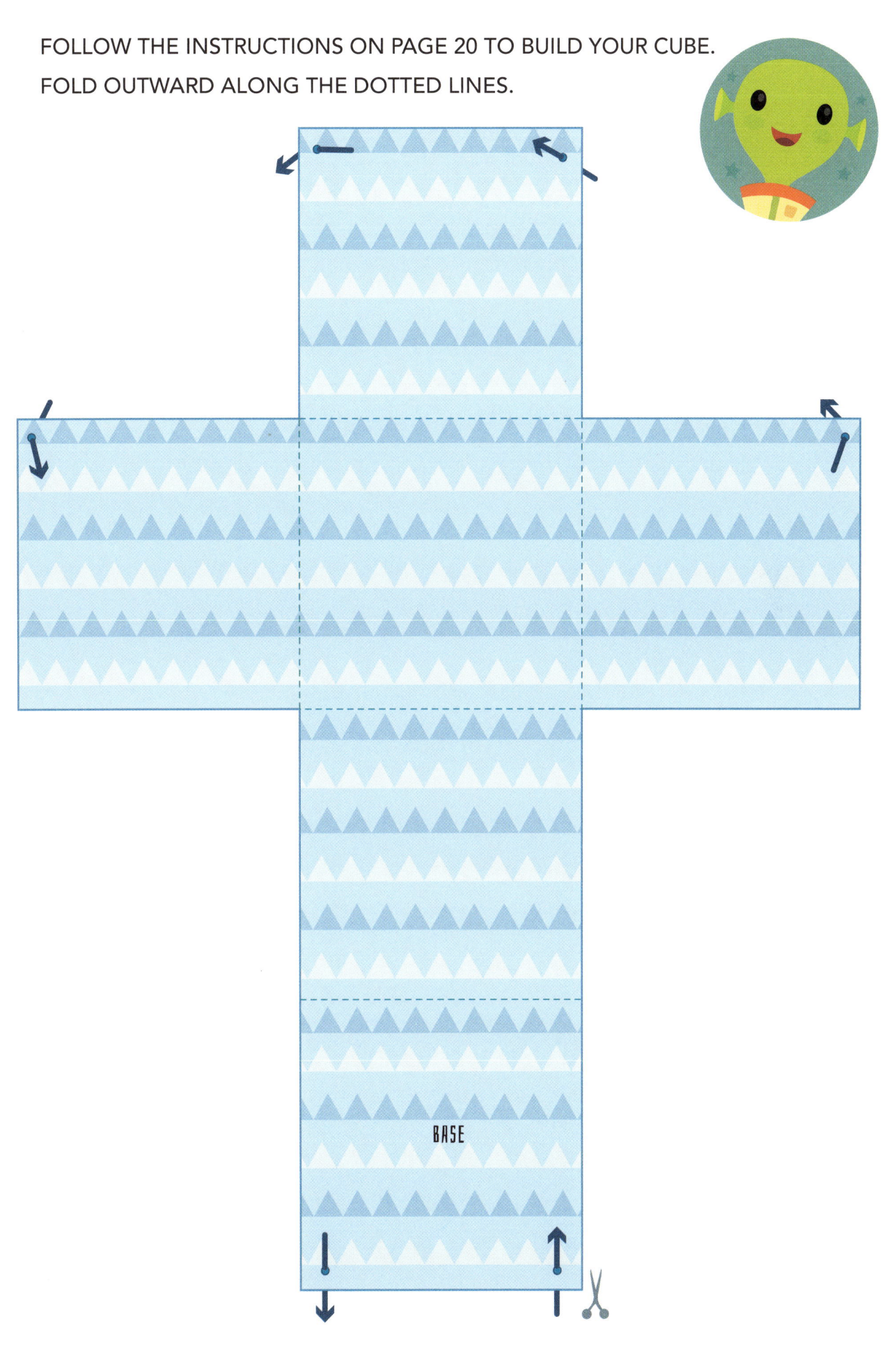

AND NOW, 3D!

ONCE YOU HAVE CUT OUT THE TETRAHEDRON AND THE CUBE FROM THE PREVIOUS PAGES, LAY THEM OUT HORIZONTALLY ON THIS PAGE, AS SHOWN IN THE GREEN IMAGES BELOW. THEN GLUE THEIR BASES WHERE SHOWN. THREAD THE STRINGS THROUGH, FOLLOWING THE INSTRUCTIONS, AND PULL IN THE DIRECTION OF THE ARROW. YOUR SOLIDS WILL TAKE SHAPE!

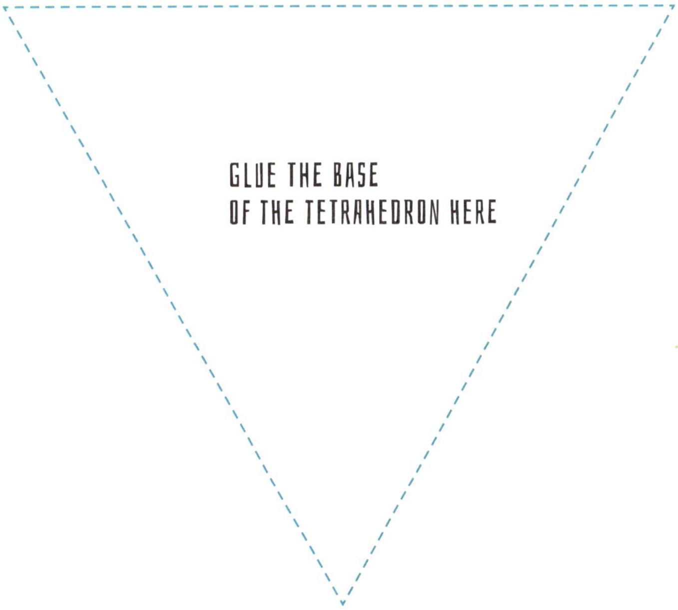

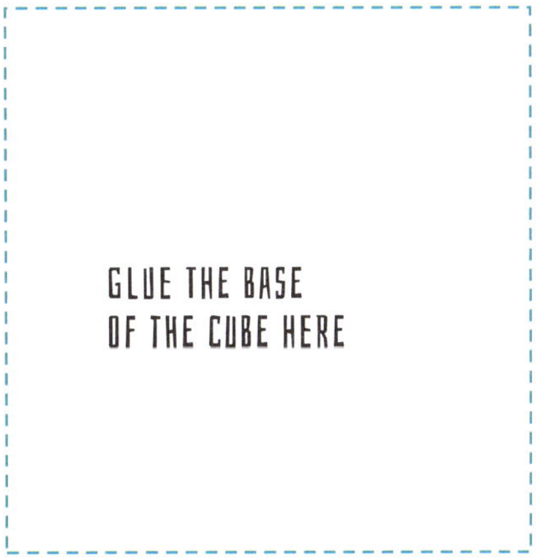

GLUE THE BASE
OF THE TETRAHEDRON HERE

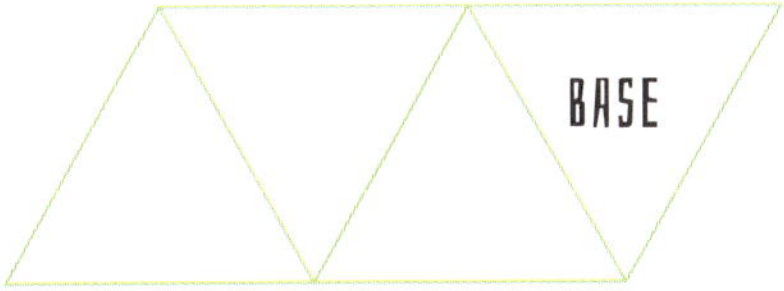

BASE

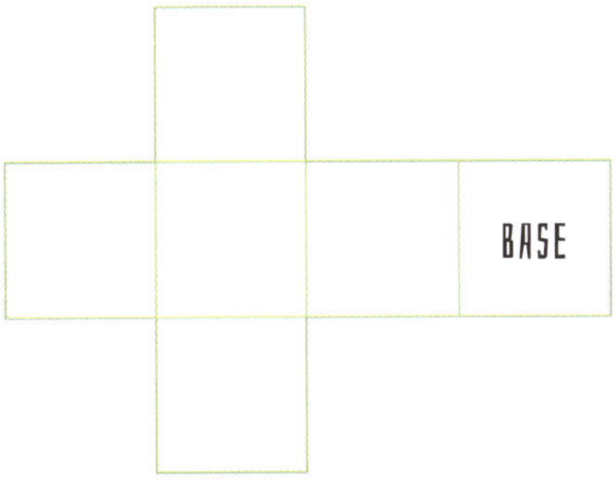

GLUE THE BASE
OF THE CUBE HERE

BASE

25

HOW MANY CAN YOU SEE?

A MESSAGE FROM THE DELTA-GAMMA QUADRANT HAS ARRIVED. IT READS:

HOW MANY SQUARES DO YOU SEE HERE?

ACCEPT THE CHALLENGE AND START COUNTING.
THE SQUARES ARE DIFFERENT SIZES, SO CONCENTRATE AND COUNT CAREFULLY!

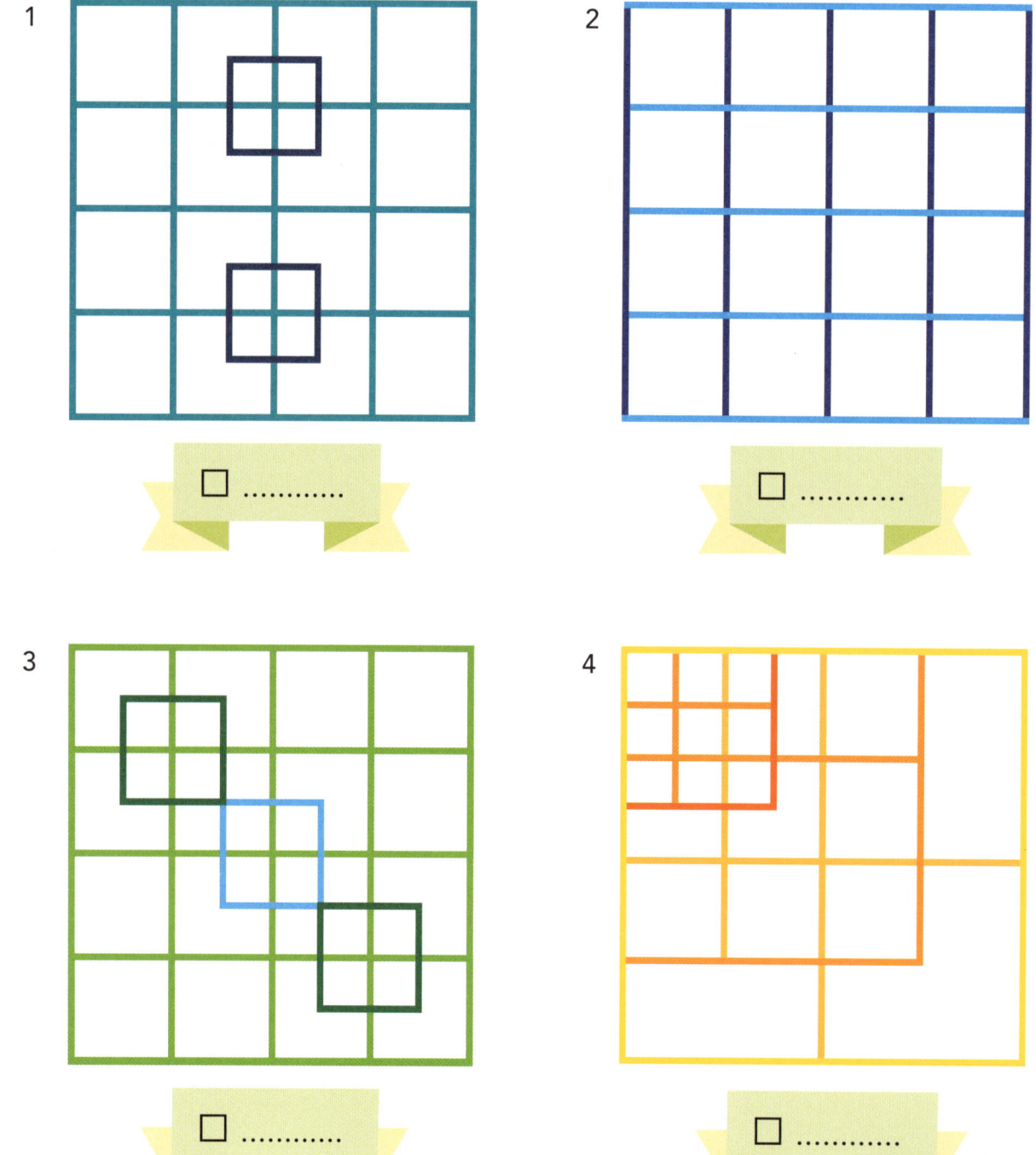

HOW MANY TRIANGLES CAN YOU SEE IN THESE FIGURES?

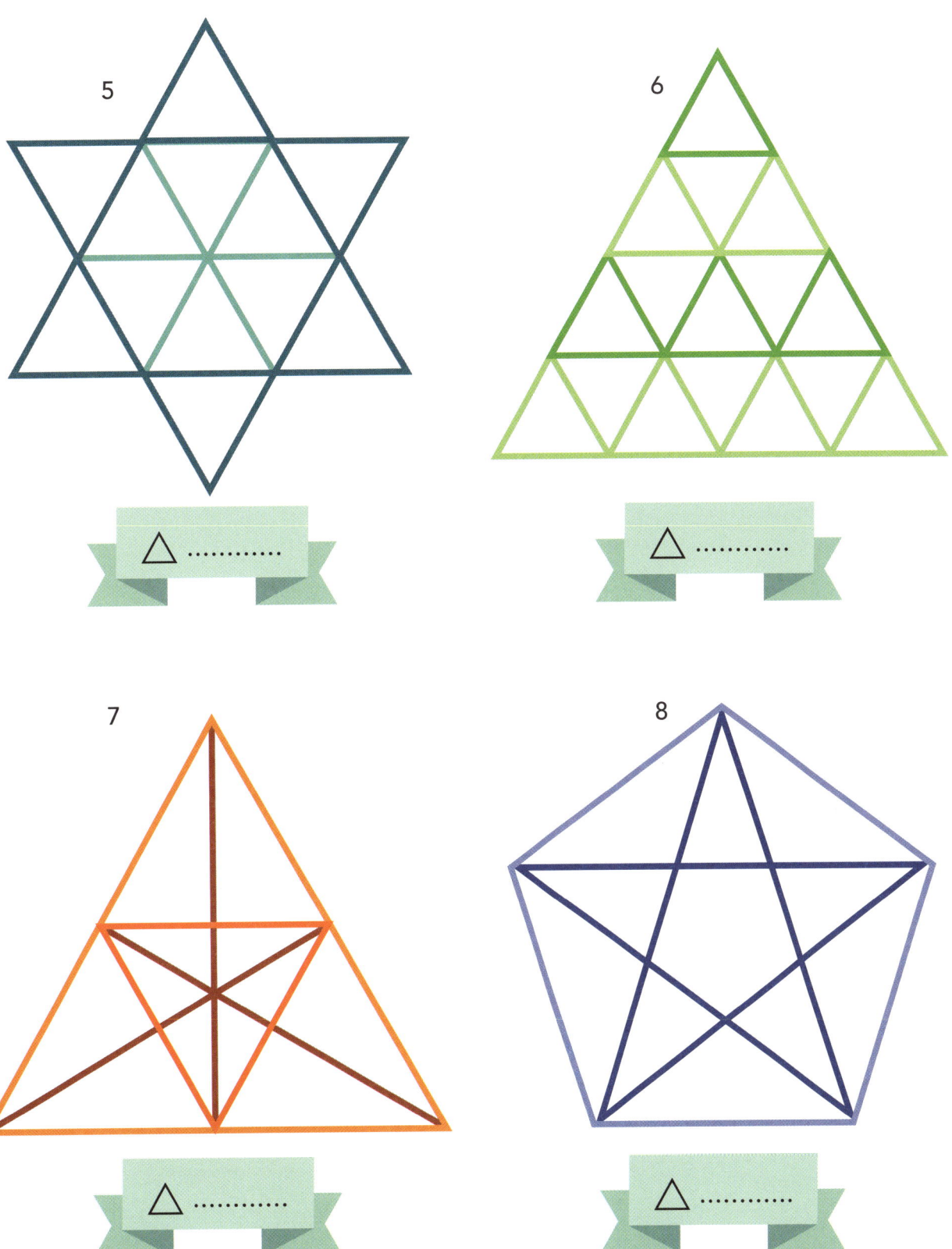

LET'S TRY AGAIN!

HOW MANY TRIANGLES AND HOW MANY SQUARES CAN YOU COUNT IN THESE FIGURES?

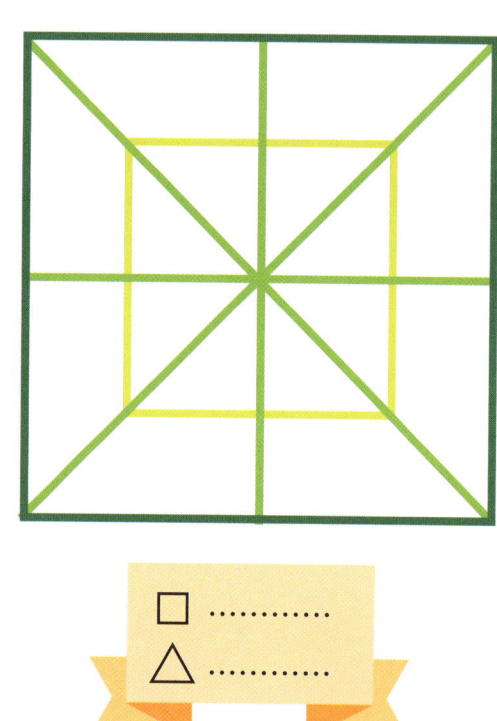

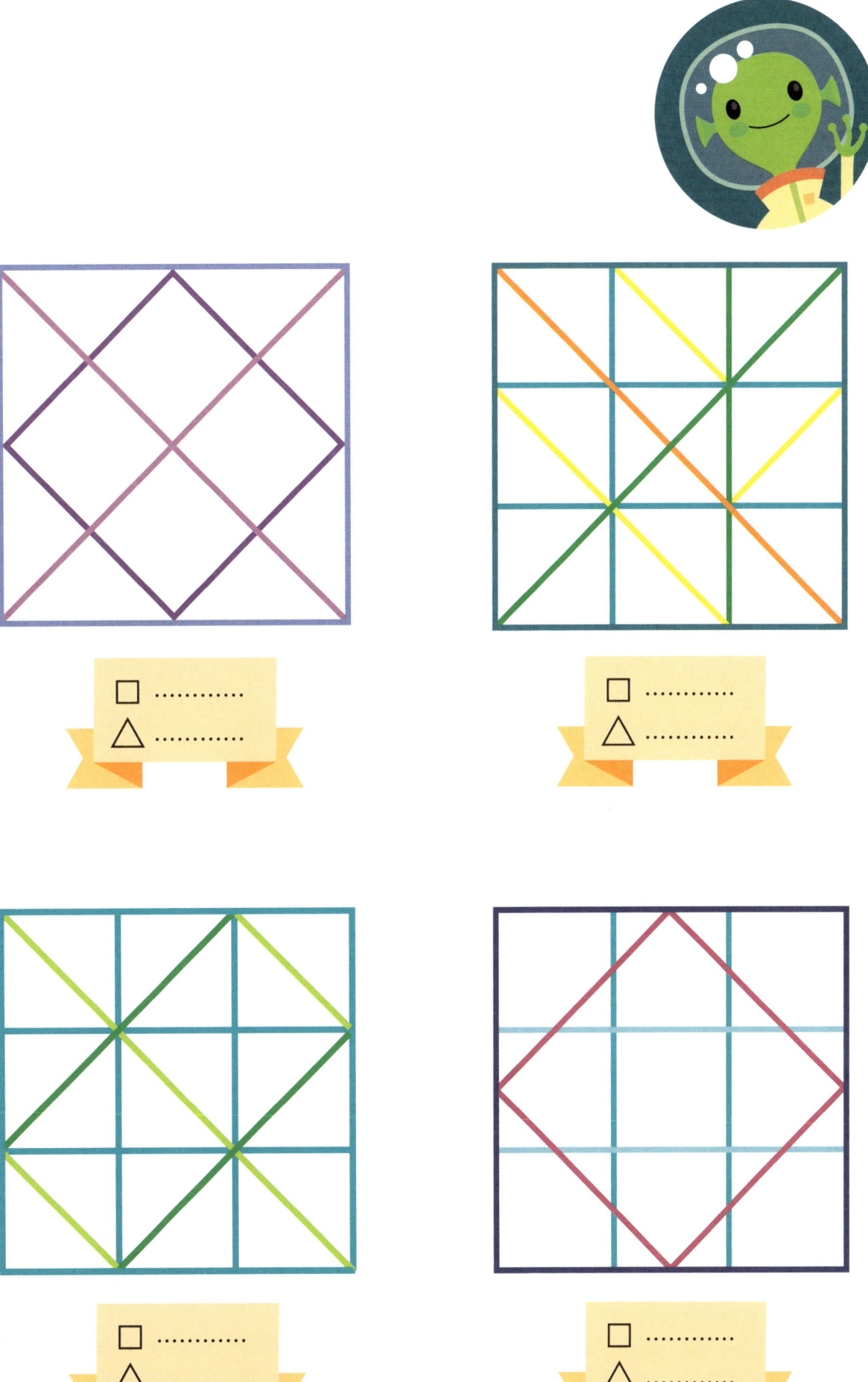

THE CELESTIAL CREATOR OF PLANETS

THE CELESTIAL CREATOR OF PLANETS IS GRAPPLING WITH A NEW PLANET-ELEVATING MACHINE THAT WORKS THANKS TO A COGWHEEL SYSTEM. IT IS FUNDAMENTAL TO UNDERSTAND WHICH DIRECTION EACH WHEEL TURNS IN ORDER TO KNOW WHICH PLANETS WILL BE RAISED!

THE ARROWS SHOW YOU THE DIRECTION IN WHICH EACH COGWHEEL TURNS.

LOOK CLOSELY AT THE COGWHEELS TO UNDERSTAND HOW THEY WORK.

WHICH PLANETS WILL BE RAISED?

THE TANGRAM COMETS

THE TANGRAM COMETS ARE INHABITED BY STRANGE CREATURES WHO HAVE ONLY 2 DIMENSIONS!
THEY ARE COMPLETELY DIFFERENT FROM, FOR EXAMPLE, A CUBE OR A BALL, WHICH HAVE 3 DIMENSIONS.

THE CREATURES WHO LIVE ON THESE COMETS ARE QUITE QUIRKY, HONESTLY.
THEY ARE BLACK ALL OVER AND HAVE PARTICULAR SHAPES.

THESE STRANGE FIGURES ARE
CREATED WITH ONLY THESE 7 PIECES:

TWO LARGE TRIANGLES,
A MEDIUM TRIANGLE,
TWO SMALL TRIANGLES,
A SQUARE, AND
A PARALLELOGRAM.

ON THE LAST PAGES OF THE BOOK,
YOU WILL FIND THE TANGRAM
STICKERS, WITH WHICH YOU CAN
TRY AND BUILD THE FIGURES!

CAN YOU FIGURE OUT HOW THESE SEVEN PIECES FIT TOGETHER? LOOK AT THE EXAMPLE OF THE CAT BELOW. THEN GUESS HOW TO PLACE THE TANGRAM'S SHAPES IN ORDER TO CREATE OTHER ANIMALS, WHICH ARE COLORED HERE TO HELP YOU. DRAW LINES WITH A PENCIL ON EACH FIGURE TO DISCOVER ITS STRUCTURE.

33

THE PLANET OF ASTROTAXIS

WE HAVE ARRIVED AT A BIG CITY WITH PARALLEL AND PERPENDICULAR STREETS. HERE, THE INHABITANTS MOVE AROUND ONLY IN ASTROTAXIS!

THE DISTANCE BETWEEN 2 POINTS CAN BE OBTAINED BY ADDING THE HORIZONTAL SEGMENTS TO THE VERTICAL SEGMENTS. THERE MAY BE MORE THAN ONE ROUTE, WITH PATHS OF THE SAME LENGTH.

FOR EXAMPLE, IN THE IMAGE BELOW, YOU CAN SEE THAT THE ASTROTAXI DISTANCES IN RED, BLUE, AND GREEN, BETWEEN POINTS **A** AND **B**, FOLLOW DIFFERENT PATHS BUT THEY ARE ARE OF THE SAME LENGTH. THAT'S BECAUSE THEY ARE MADE FROM THE SUM OF 16 **SEGMENT UNITS**. THESE ROUTES SHOW THE POSSIBLE **MINIMUM** TAXI DISTANCES—THAT IS, THE SHORTEST ROUTES THAT GO FROM A TO B.

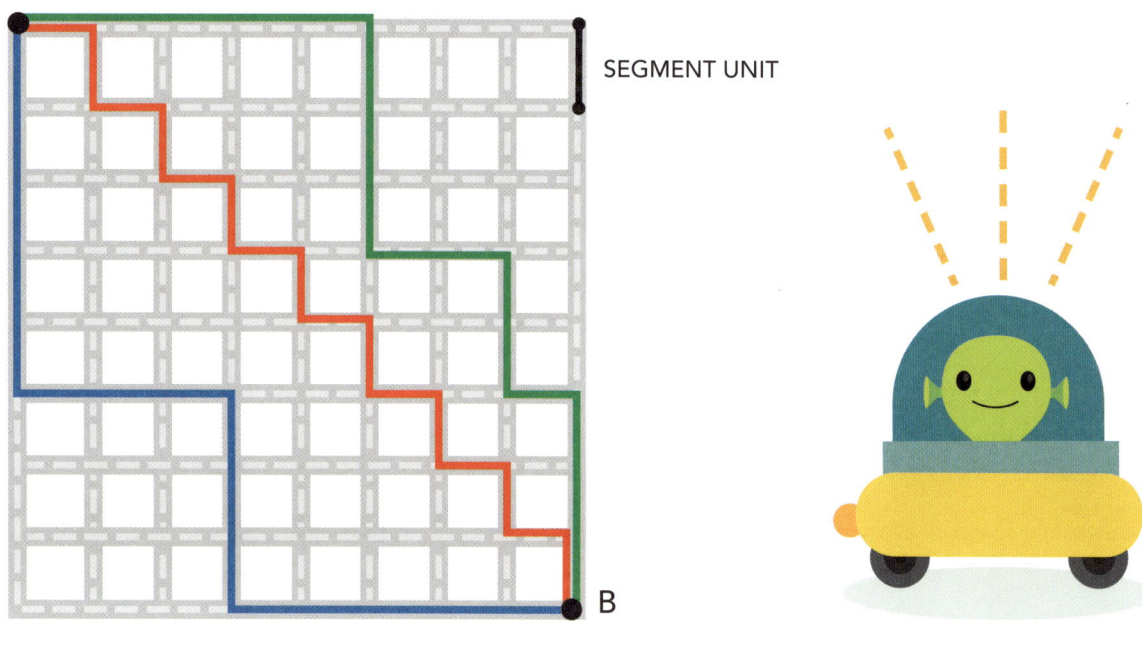

HOW MANY UNITS DO THE THREE ASTROTAXI ROUTES IN THIS IMAGE TRAVEL BETWEEN POINTS **C** AND **D**? WHICH OF THESE IS THE SHORTEST?

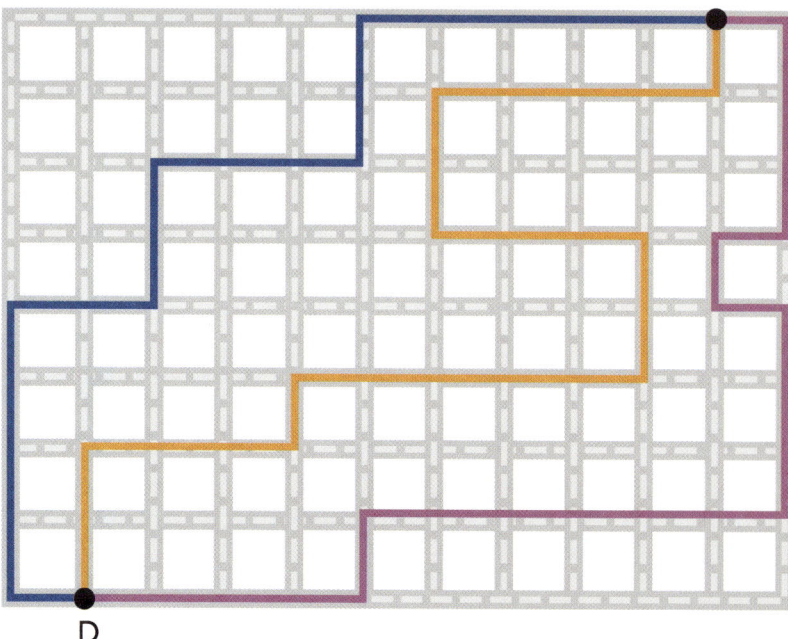

WHAT IS THE TAXI'S MINIMUM DISTANCE FOR GOING FROM E TO F? CAN YOU FIND AT LEAST THREE DIFFERENT ROUTES?

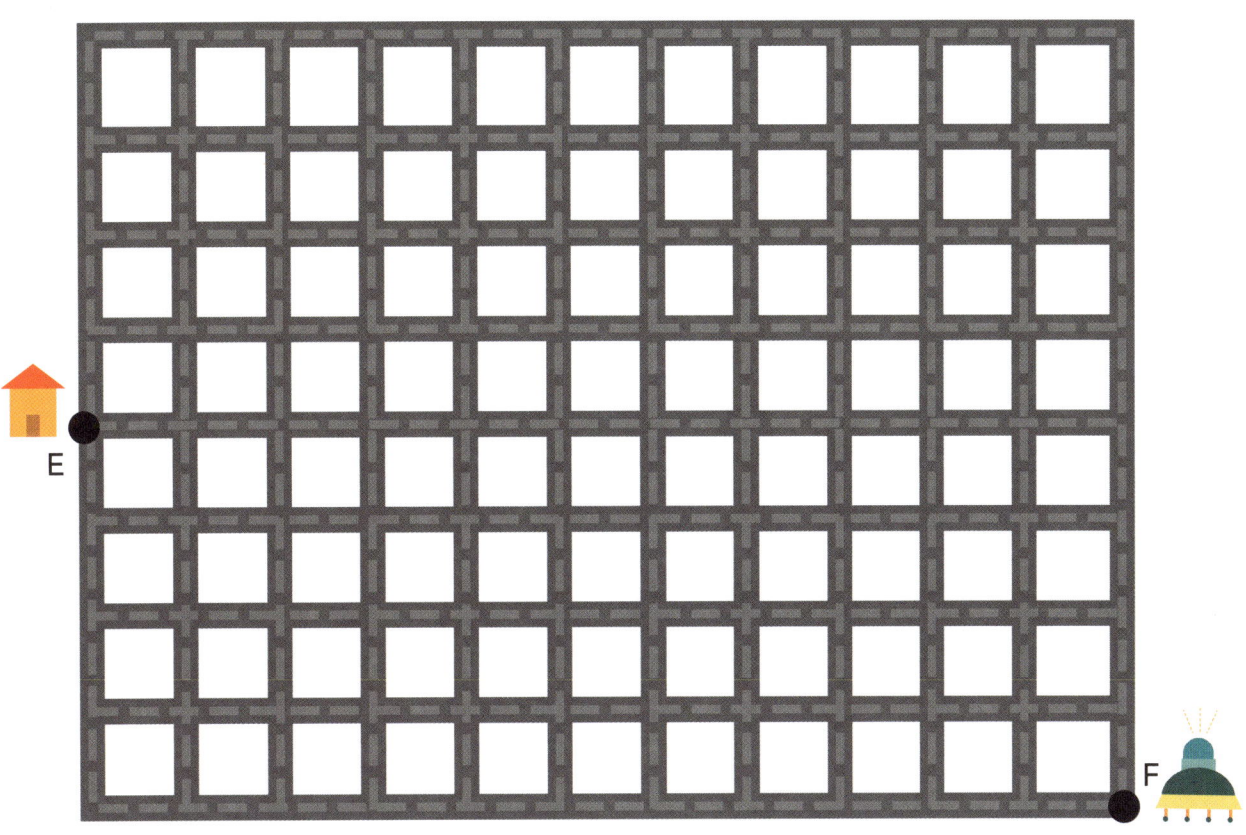

AND BETWEEN G AND H?

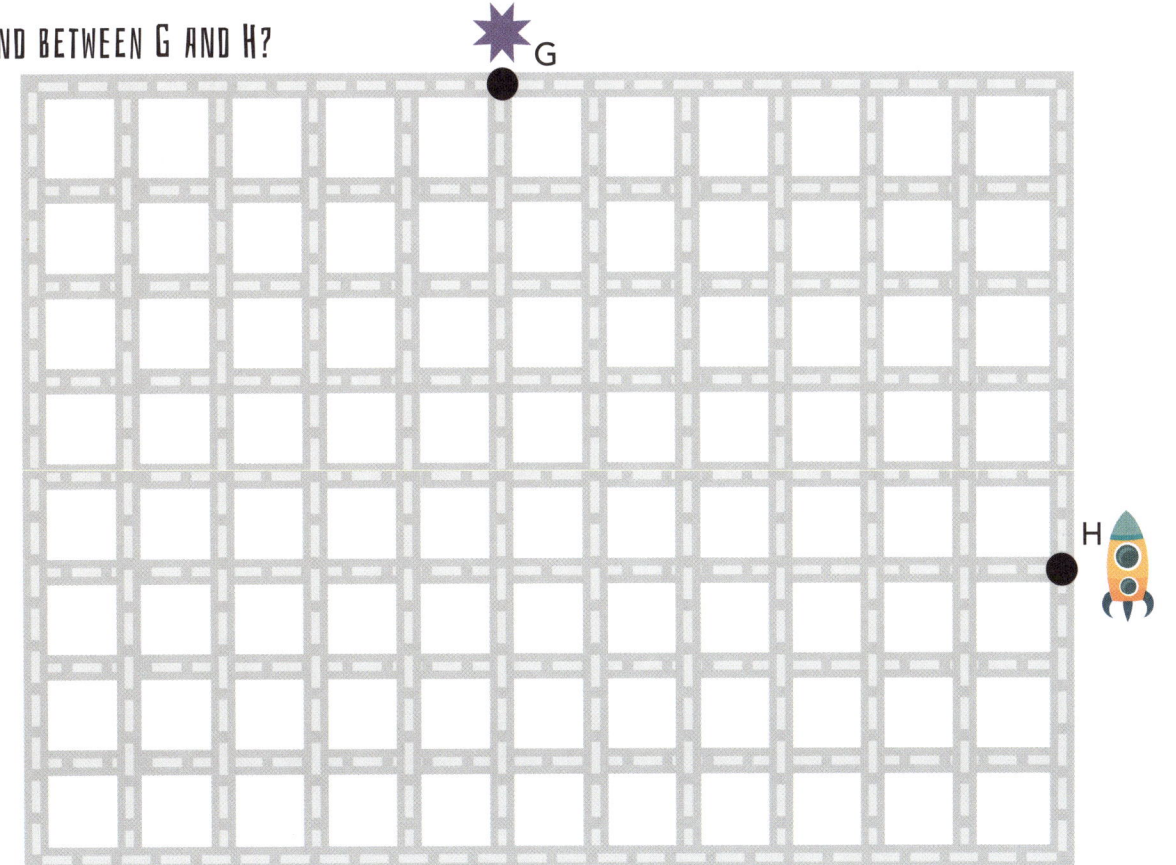

ASTEROIDS WITH A MIRROR

OH NO! WE ARE STUCK IN AN ASTEROID TRAFFIC JAM!
EACH ASTEROID HAS A PARTICULAR SHAPE: THEY ARE TWO-DIMENSIONAL, FLAT FIGURES. WE MUST GET THROUGH THIS BARRIER TO REACH MY SHUTTLE, WHICH IS LOCATED ON THE OTHER SIDE. BUT WHAT CAN WE DO?

HOW CAN WE MOVE THEM?

HERE IS A SUREFIRE WAY: **AXIAL REFLECTIONS**.
ACCORDING TO THE RULES, EACH FIGURE CAN MOVE BUT IT DOES NOT CHANGE SHAPE! TO FLIP A FIGURE, WE WILL NEED AN AXIS OF SYMMETRY, LIKE THE BLUE LINE YOU SEE BELOW. WE MUST MEASURE THE DISTANCE OF EACH POINT FROM THE **AXIS OF SYMMETRY** AND THEN MARK THE SAME DISTANCE ON THE OTHER SIDE OF THE AXIS.

LET'S START FROM POINT **A**. ITS DISTANCE FROM THE AXIS IS 2. WE COUNT THE SAME DISTANCE ON THE OTHER SIDE OF THE AXIS AND MARK THE SYMMETRY POINT **A1**. AFTER OBTAINING ALL THE POINTS WITH THIS SYSTEM, WE'LL JUST NEED TO CONNECT THEM TO OBTAIN THE SYMMETRICAL FIGURE.

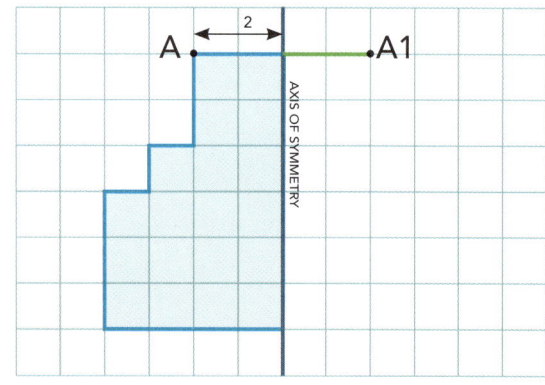
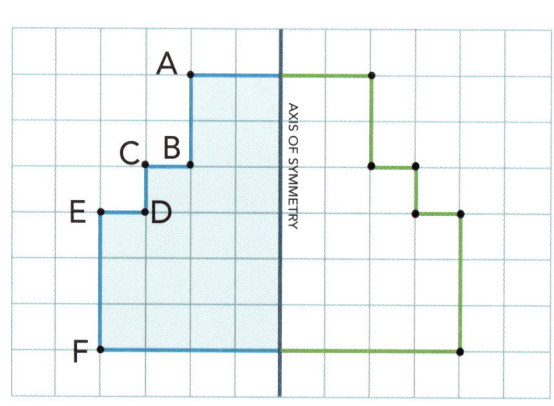

FOLLOWING THIS RULE, CAN YOU TURN THE ASTEROIDS? PRACTICE BY MOVING THE PINK AND YELLOW ASTEROIDS IN THE PACES BELOW, TURNING THEM OVER THE AXIS OF SYMMETRY.

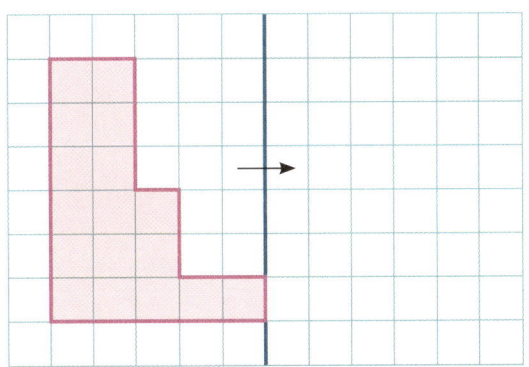
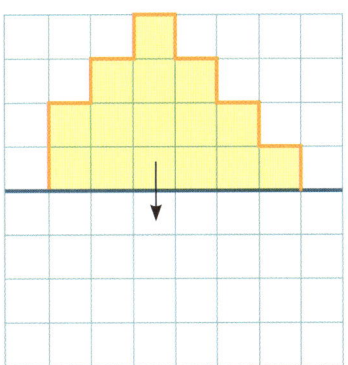

LET'S GET BACK TO THE ASTEROID JAM! MOVE THE NECESSARY ASTEROIDS TO CREATE AN OPENING IN THE BARRIER AND REACH MY SHUTTLE. THE OPENING MUST BE AS BIG AS ME—THAT IS, 2 BY 2 SQUARES. WORK CAREFULLY: YOU CAN ONLY MOVE THE BLUE ASTEROIDS; **THE GREEN ONES CANNOT BE MOVED**.
YOU CHOOSE WHERE TO PLACE THE AXIS OF SYMMETRY!

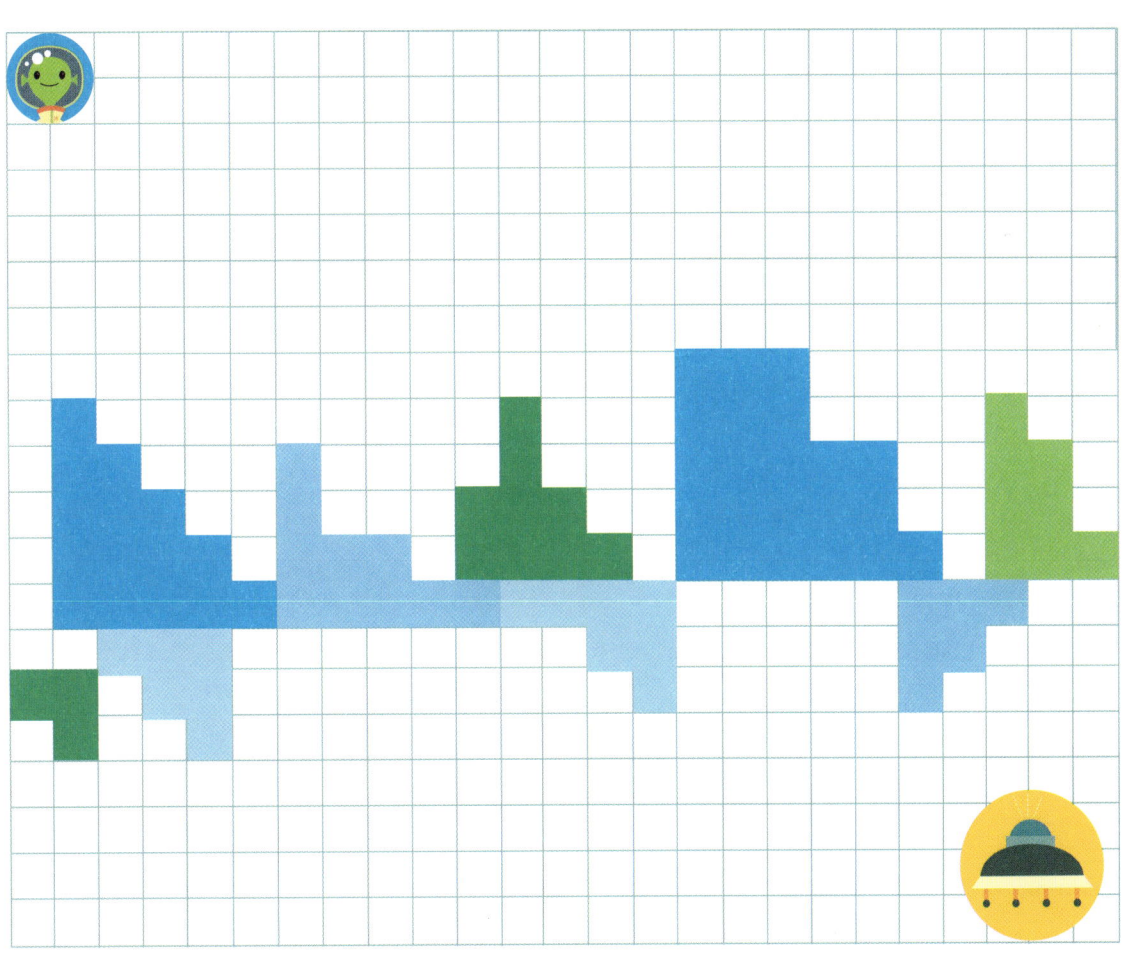

37

LET'S PLAY SOME MORE!

LOOK AT THE EXAMPLE: HERE, THE AXIS OF SYMMETRY IS DETACHED FROM THE FIGURES.

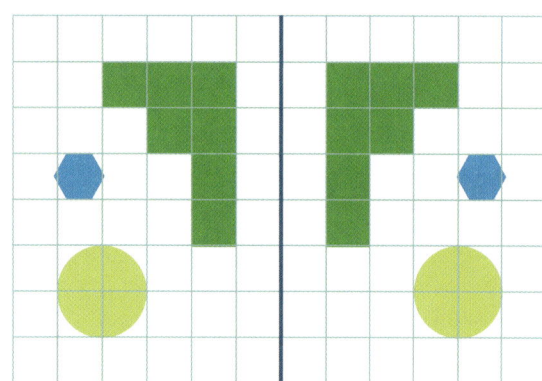

NOW, TAKE THE STICKERS FROM THE BACK OF THE BOOK, BRING THEM NEAR THE AXIS OF SYMMETRY, AND WITH A PENCIL COMPLETE THEIR AXIAL REFLECTIONS.

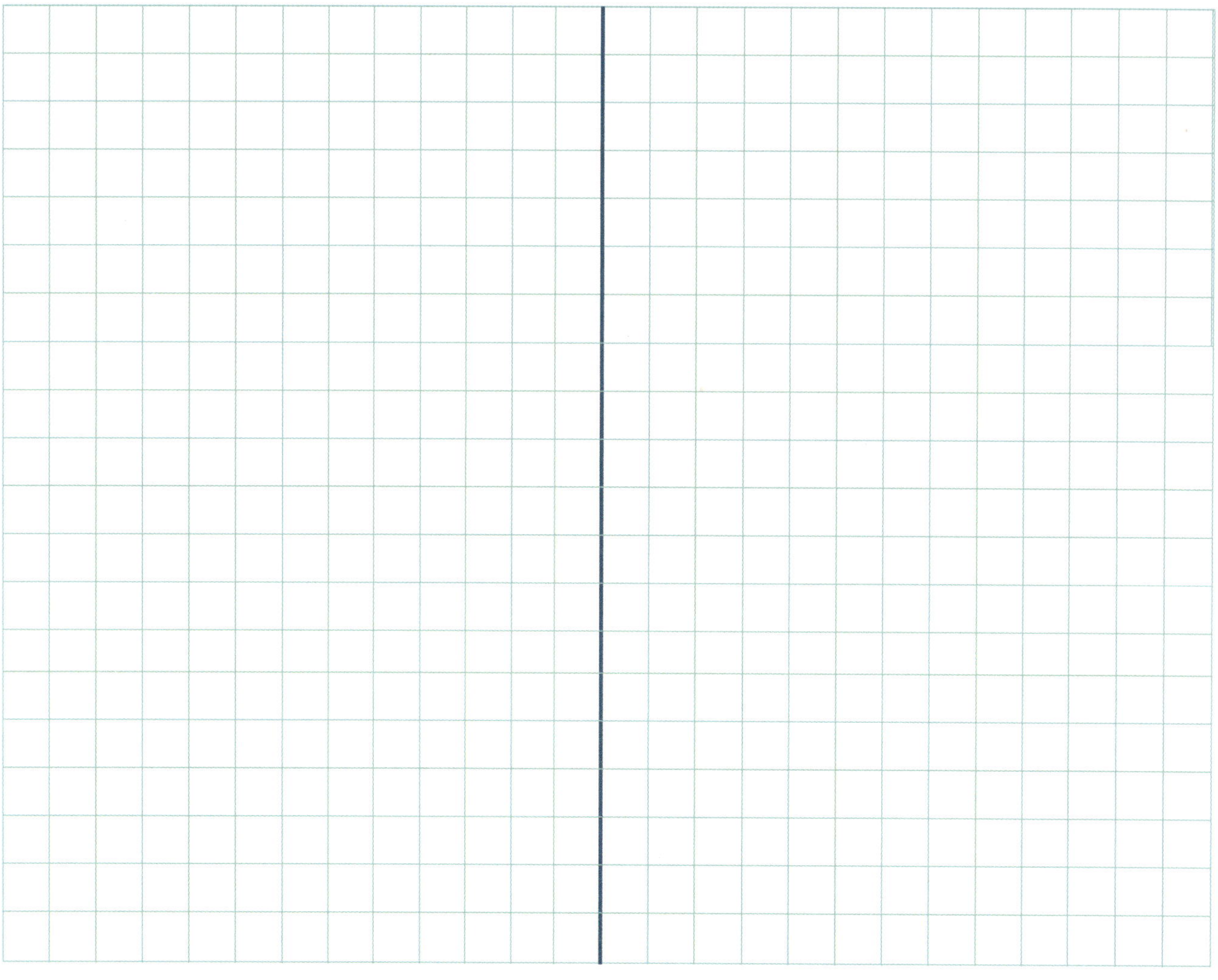

ROTATION

ROTATION IS THE ACTION OF ROTATING A FIGURE AROUND A POINT, CALLED A CENTER OF ROTATION. THE ANGLE OF ROTATION INDICATES HOW MANY DEGREES THE FIGURE MUST ROTATE AROUND THE AXIS.

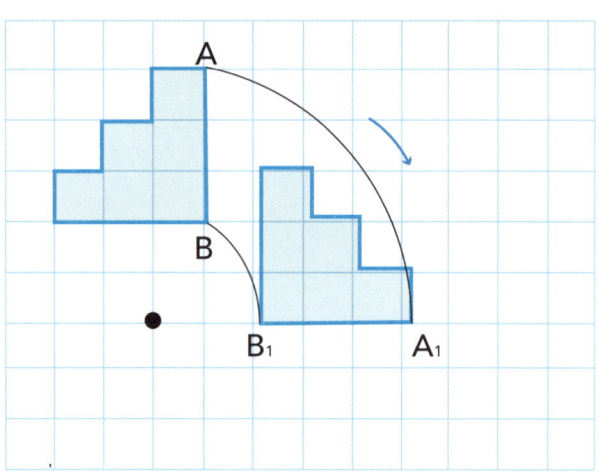

CHOOSE ONE OR MORE STICKERS THAT YOU LIKE ON THE LAST PAGES OF THE BOOK AND PUT THEM ONTO THE SQUARES. THEN, CHOOSE A CENTER OF ROTATION AND AN ANGLE AND HAVE FUN ROTATING THE FIGURE AND DRAWING IT IN THE POSITION THAT IT WILL HAVE AFTER ROTATION.
COLOR IT, THEN TRY OUT OTHER SHAPES!

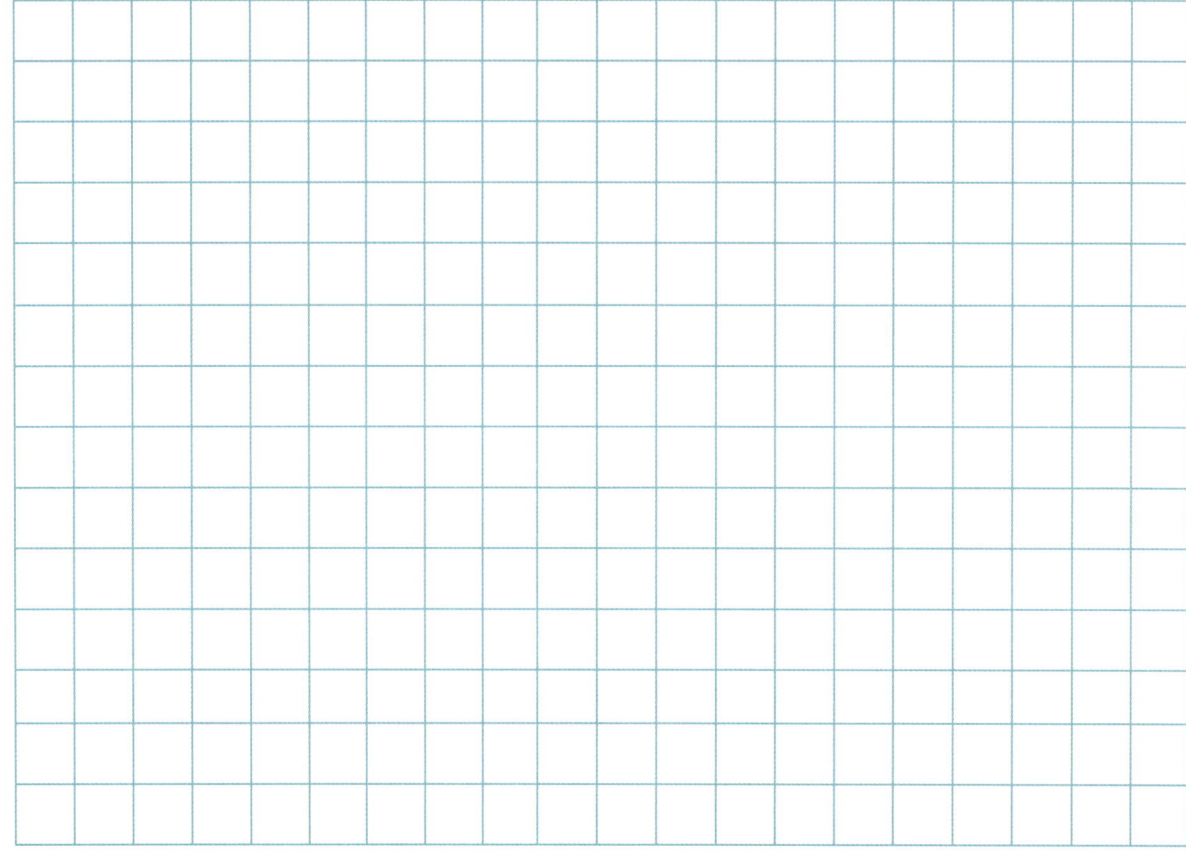

TRANSLATION

TRANSLATION IS THE MOVEMENT OF A FIGURE FROM ONE POINT TO ANOTHER; ALL ITS POINTS MOVE IN THE SAME DIRECTION, CALLED THE **VECTOR**, INDICATED BELOW BY THE ARROWS. THIS MOVEMENT CAN BE DONE VIA A HORIZONTAL, VERTICAL, OR DIAGONAL LINE.

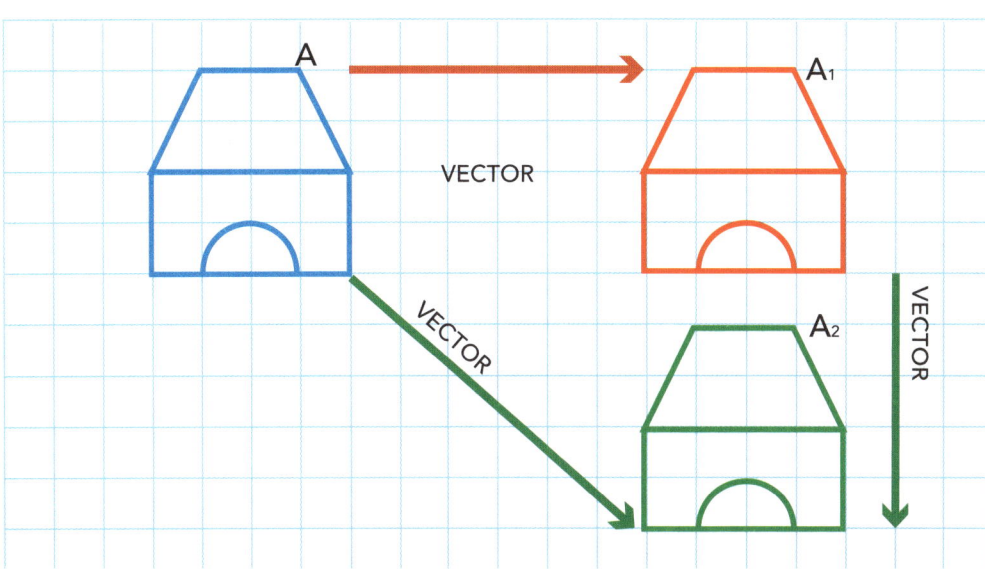

CHOOSE ONE OR MORE STICKERS THAT YOU LIKE ON THE LAST PAGES OF THE BOOK, THEN PUT THEM ONTO THE SQUARES. CHOOSE A VECTOR AND MOVE THE WHOLE FIGURE ACCORDINGLY. COLOR IT, THEN TRY OUT OTHER SHAPES!

THE ETERNAL PATH OF THE WANGA MANGAS

HAVE YOU EVER THOUGHT OF TRAVELING AROUND SPACE BUT ALWAYS RETURNING TO THE SAME STARTING POINT? IT DOESN'T MATTER HOW FAST OR SLOW YOU WALK, YOUR PATH WILL ALWAYS TAKE YOU RIGHT BACK TO THE SAME POINT.
THE **WANGA MANGAS**, INHABITANTS OF THE **MOEBIUS STRIP**, A MONODIMENSIONAL SURFACE WITH ONLY ONE FACE, LIVE THIS LIFE! IN THEIR WORLD THERE IS NEVER AN ABOVE, NOR A BELOW!
ON THE OPPOSITE PAGE YOU'LL FIND A PATTERN TO MAKE THE MOEBIUS STRIP FOR THE WANGA MANGAS TO WALK ON.
FOLLOW THESE INSTRUCTIONS.

YOU WILL NEED:
1. SCISSORS
2. GLUE OR SCOTCH TAPE

HOW TO RE-CREATE THE WANGA MANGAS' WORLD
1. CUT OUT THE RECTANGULAR STRIP.
2. ROTATE ONE OF THE ENDS OF THE STRIP 180°.
3. BRING THE TWO ENDS TOGETHER: MAKE SURE YOU PUT THE A EDGES TOGETHER AND THE B EDGES TOGETHER.
4. STICK THE TWO ENDS TOGETHER WITH A PIECE OF TAPE OR GLUE.

 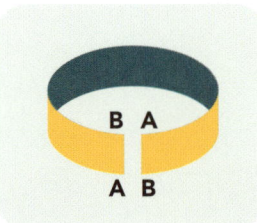  

TRY TO MOVE ALONG THE ROAD, FIRST IN THE MIDDLE AND THEN FOLLOWING JUST ONE EDGE.

DID YOU HAVE FUN?

BUILD MORE MOEBIUS STRIPS: YOU'LL FIND THE STICKERS ON THE LAST PAGES OF THE BOOK!

STELLAR MAPS

WE HAVE ALMOST REACHED THE END OF OUR JOURNEY. IT'S TIME TO FILL OUT THE LOGBOOK WITH THE STELLAR MAPS, DIVIDED INTO QUADRANTS, THAT WE HAVE BEEN FOLLOWING.
WE NEED TO COLOR THEM ACCORDING TO THE RULES OF THE MANUAL. LOOK AT THE EXAMPLE BELOW.

THE THEOREM OF THE FOUR COLORS

A STELLAR MAP DIVIDED INTO REGIONS ALWAYS NEEDS AT LEAST **FOUR DIFFERENT COLORS TO MAKE SURE AREAS ADJACENT TO ONE ANOTHER ARE OF A DIFFERENT COLOR.** TWO REGIONS ARE SAID TO BE ADJACENT IF THEY HAVE AT LEAST ONE BORDER IN COMMON.

IT'S YOUR TURN: INSTRUCTIONS FOR COLORING

1. GET YOURSELF SOME COLORED PENCILS OR MARKERS.
2. USE THE COLOR RED TO COLOR IN ONE OF THE QUADRANTS.
3. COLOR AS MANY OF THE QUADRANTS AS POSSIBLE IN RED, BUT BE CAREFUL: NO QUADRANT COLORED **RED** CAN BORDER ON ANOTHER RED QUADRANT.
4. WHEN YOU CAN'T FIND ANY MORE QUADRANTS TO COLOR RED, START COLORING QUADRANTS WITH THE COLOR **BLUE**.
5. COLOR AS MANY QUADRANTS AS YOU CAN FOLLOWING THE SAME RULE: NO QUADRANT NEXT TO A BLUE QUADRANT CAN BE BLUE.
6. REPEAT FROM STEP 1, CHANGING COLORS UNTIL ALL THE QUADRANTS ARE COLORED IN.

CAN YOU USE JUST 4 COLORS FOLLOWING THE INSTRUCTIONS?
CAN YOU DO THE SAME WITH JUST 3?

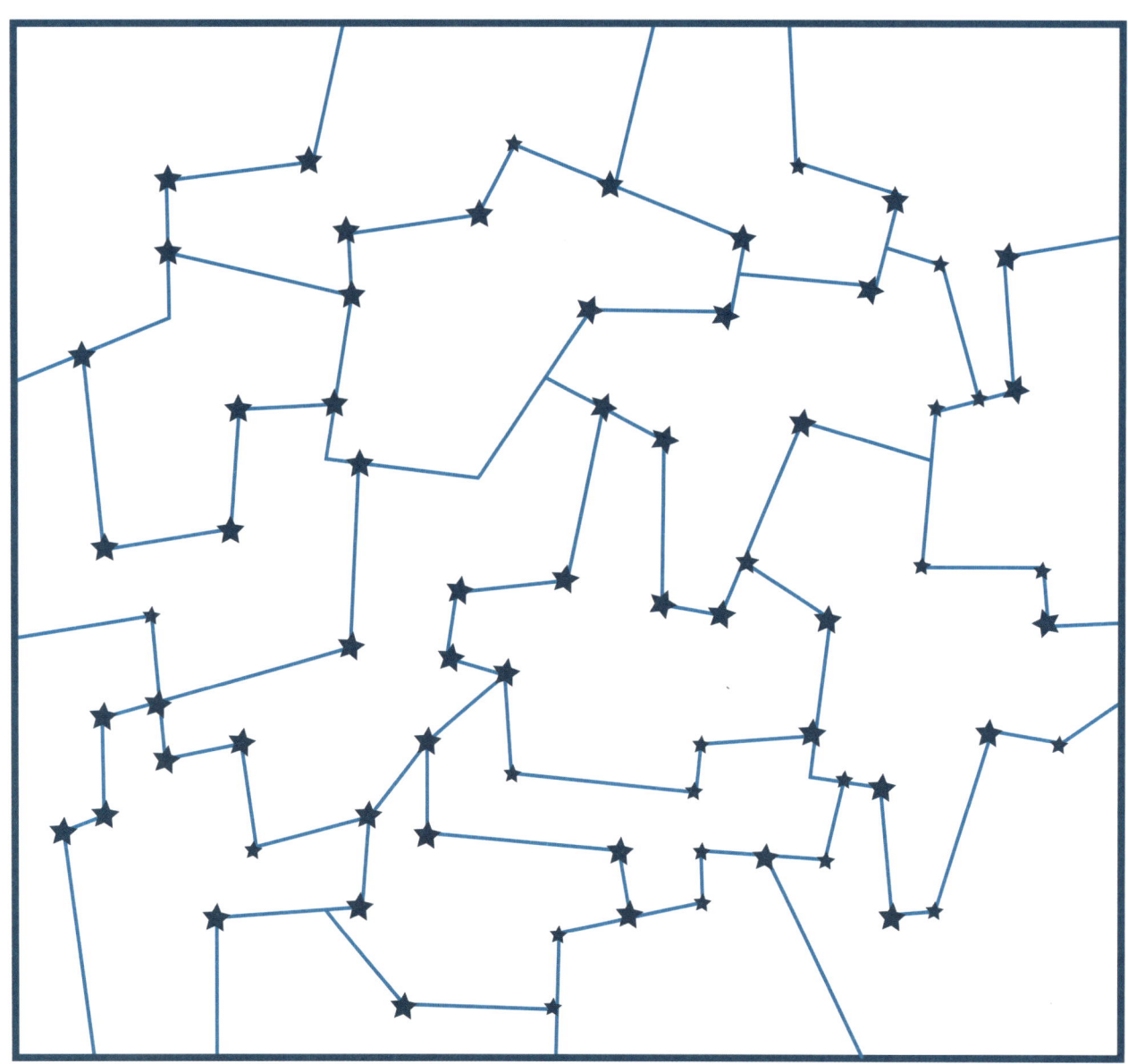

TRY AGAIN!

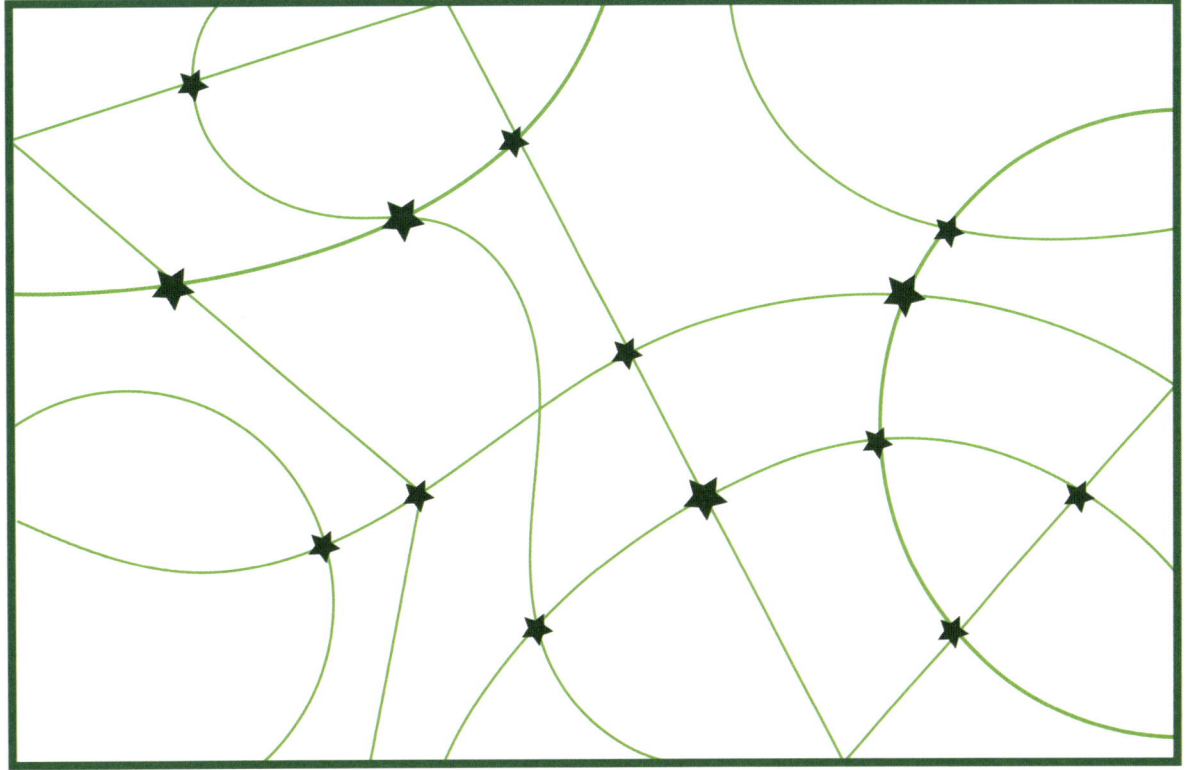

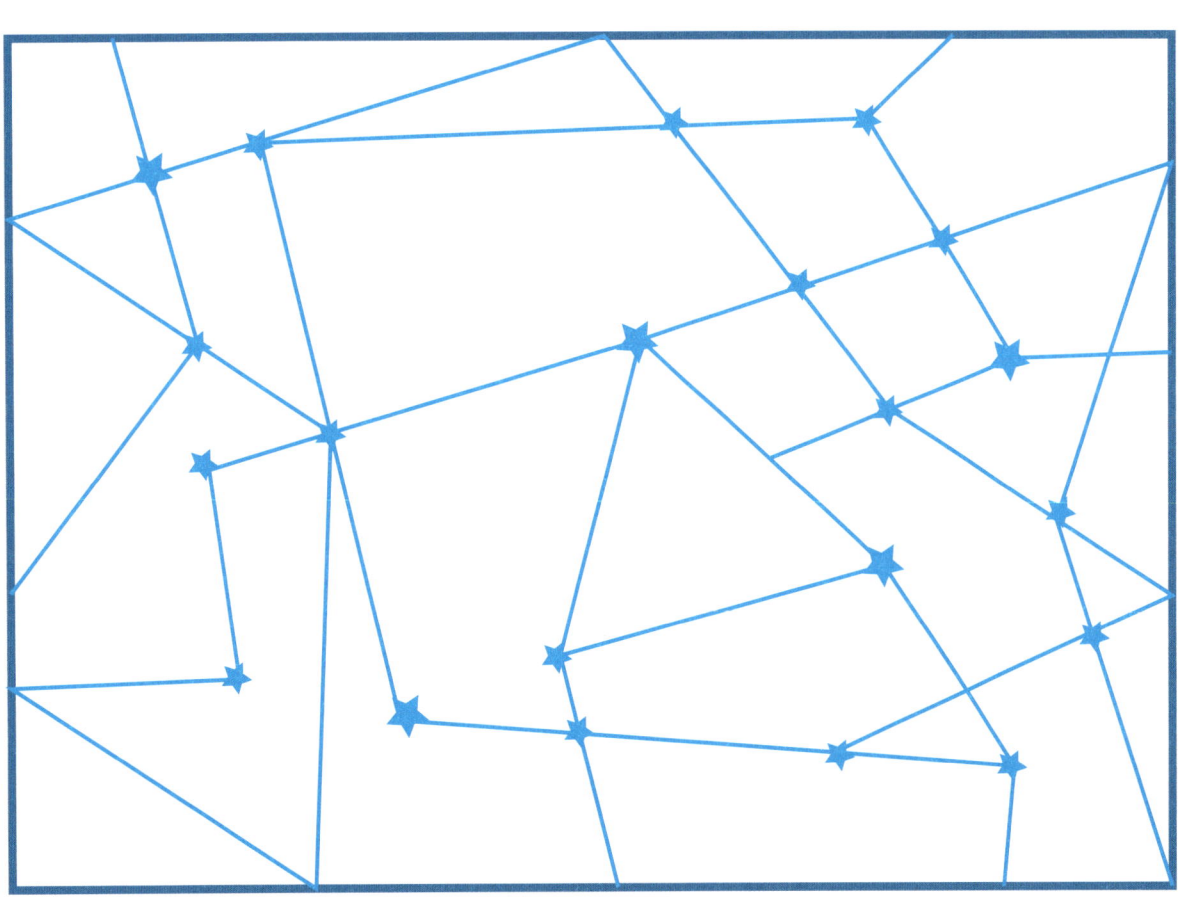

WOCH, THE MONOCLIMATE PLANET

YOU MAY COME ACROSS **MONOCLIMATE** PLANETS IN THE UNIVERSE. ON EARTH YOU HAVE SUNNY, RAINY, HOT, AND COLD DAYS, BUT ON MONOCLIMATE PLANETS THE WEATHER IS ALWAYS THE SAME! ON **WOCH** IT SNOWS EVERY SINGLE DAY!
DID YOU KNOW THAT NO TWO SNOWFLAKES ARE THE SAME? ON **WOCH**, YOU CAN FIND A REALLY SPECIAL SNOWFLAKE:
YOU CAN SEE IT UP CLOSE BELOW.
DO YOU WANT TO LEARN HOW TO MAKE IT?

YOU WILL NEED:
1. A PENCIL
2. TRIANGULAR STICKERS FROM THE BACK OF THE BOOK

INSTRUCTIONS:
1. TAKE ONE OF THE TWO LARGEST TRIANGULAR STICKERS AND STICK IT INSIDE ONE OF THE TWO LIGHT BLUE TRIANGLE OUTLINES ON THE FACING PAGE.
2. TAKE THE OTHER LARGE TRIANGULAR STICKER AND STICK IT ABOVE THE FIRST ONE SO THAT IT MATCHES UP WITH THE OTHER LIGHT BLUE OUTLINE.
3. TAKE EACH OF THE 12 SMALLER STICKERS, ONE AT A TIME, AND STICK THEM ONTO THE SPACES WITH THE DARK BLUE OUTLINES.

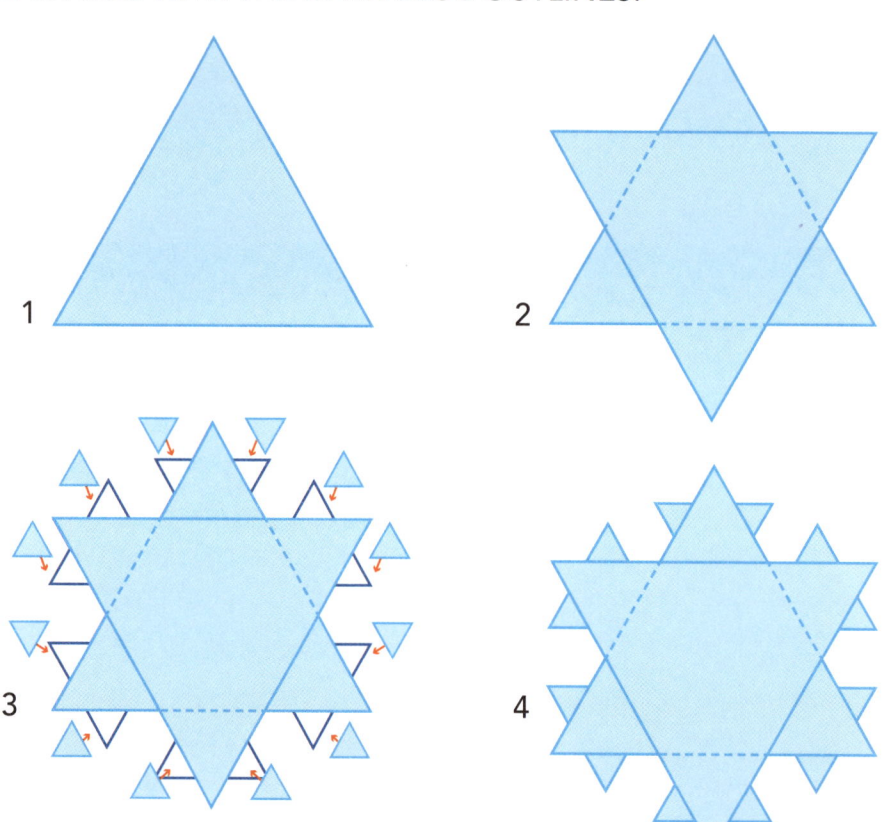

FOLLOW THE INSTRUCTIONS AND BUILD YOUR OWN BEAUTIFUL SNOWFLAKE FROM PLANET WOCH!

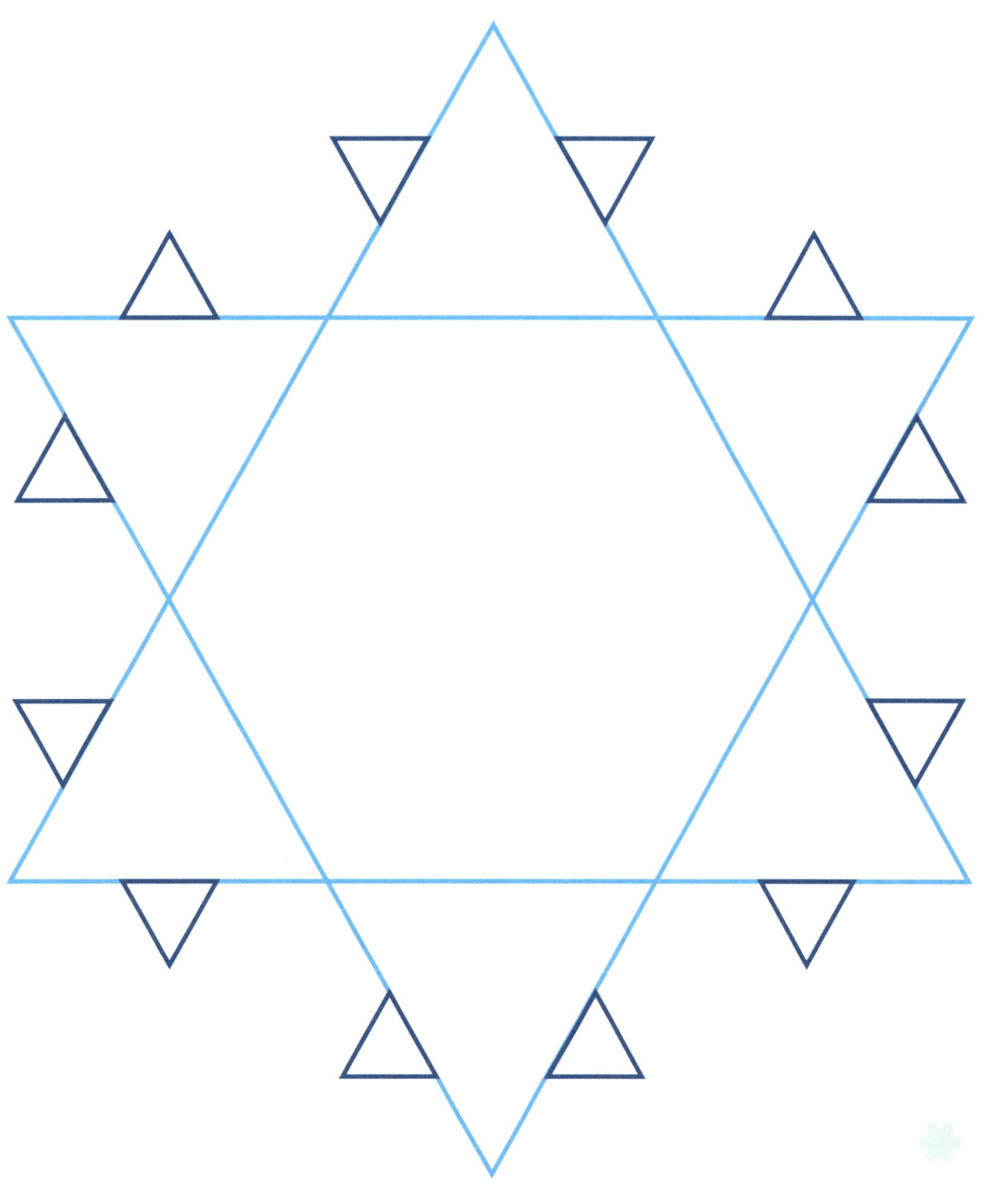

THE WORLD OF CROTON

WE HAVE GOTTEN TO THE LAST LEG OF OUR GALACTIC JOURNEY. CROTON IS AN ANCIENT PLACE INHABITED BY THE **PYTHAGORIANS**, WHO HAVE DEDICATED THEMSELVES TO STUDYING TRIANGLES, SQUARES, AND AREAS!

FIRST, OBSERVE THIS SPECIAL TRIANGLE THAT HAS A RIGHT ANGLE: IT'S CALLED A **RIGHT TRIANGLE**, AND ITS PERPENDICULAR SIDES ARE CALLED **CATHETI** (OR LEGS). THE THIRD SIDE IS CALLED THE **HYPOTENUSE**.

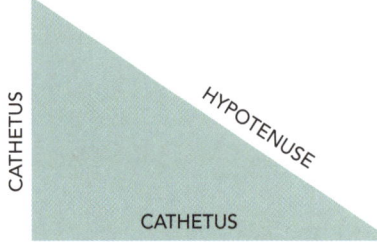

NOW YOU KNOW ABOUT RIGHT TRIANGLES. THE PYTHAGORIANS WILL BE HAPPY TO REVEAL AN ELEGANT THEOREM THAT GETS ITS NAME FROM AN ANCIENT GREEK PHILOSOPHER. JUST A MINUTE…DO YOU REMEMBER HOW TO CALCULATE THE AREA OF A SQUARE? WE SPOKE ABOUT IT ON PAGE 14.

AREA = SIDE X SIDE

WE CAN ALSO SAY THAT
AREA OF SQUARE = SIDE^2

PYTHAGORAS' THEOREM: THE SQUARE BUILT ON THE HYPOTENUSE IS EQUAL TO THE SUM OF THE SQUARES BUILT ON THE CATHETI.

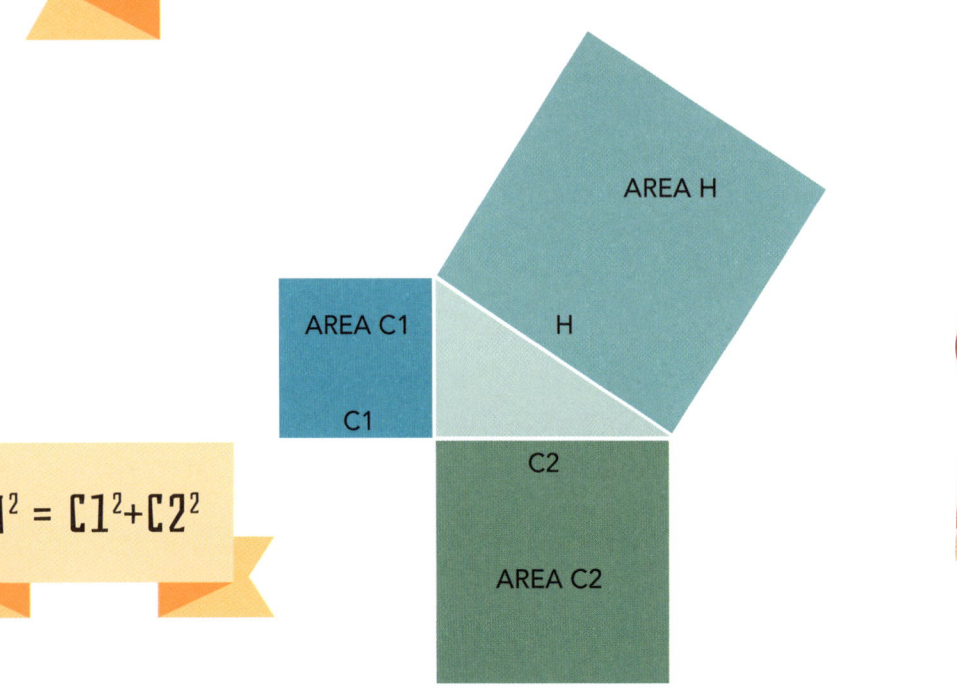

$H^2 = C1^2 + C2^2$

NOW, TRY TO SOLVE THESE PROBLEMS WITH ME!
USE THE DATA YOU HAVE TO CALCULATE THE INFORMATION NEEDED.

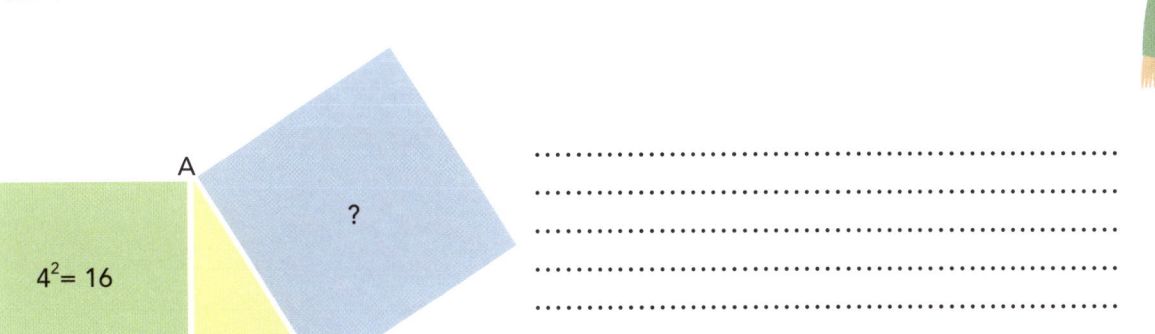

....
....
....
....
....
....

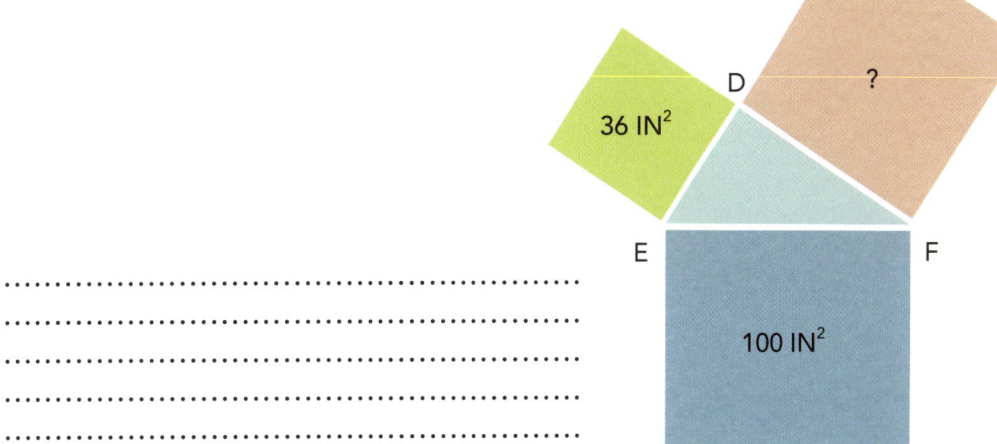

....
....
....
....
....
....

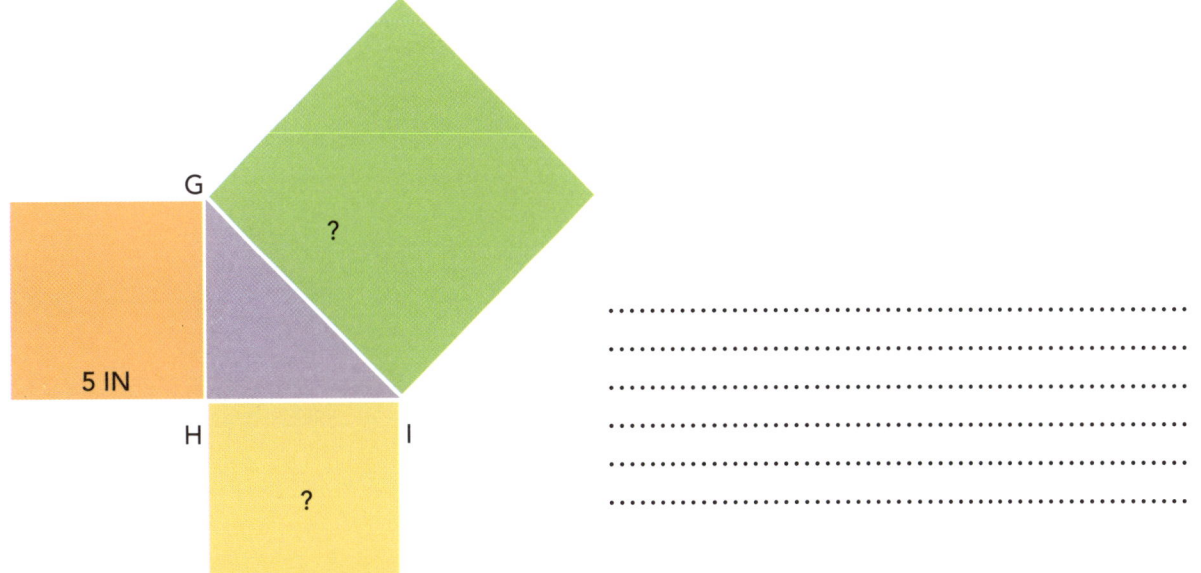

....
....
....
....
....

51

SOLUTIONS

PP. 6-7: CONSTELLATIONS AND LINES

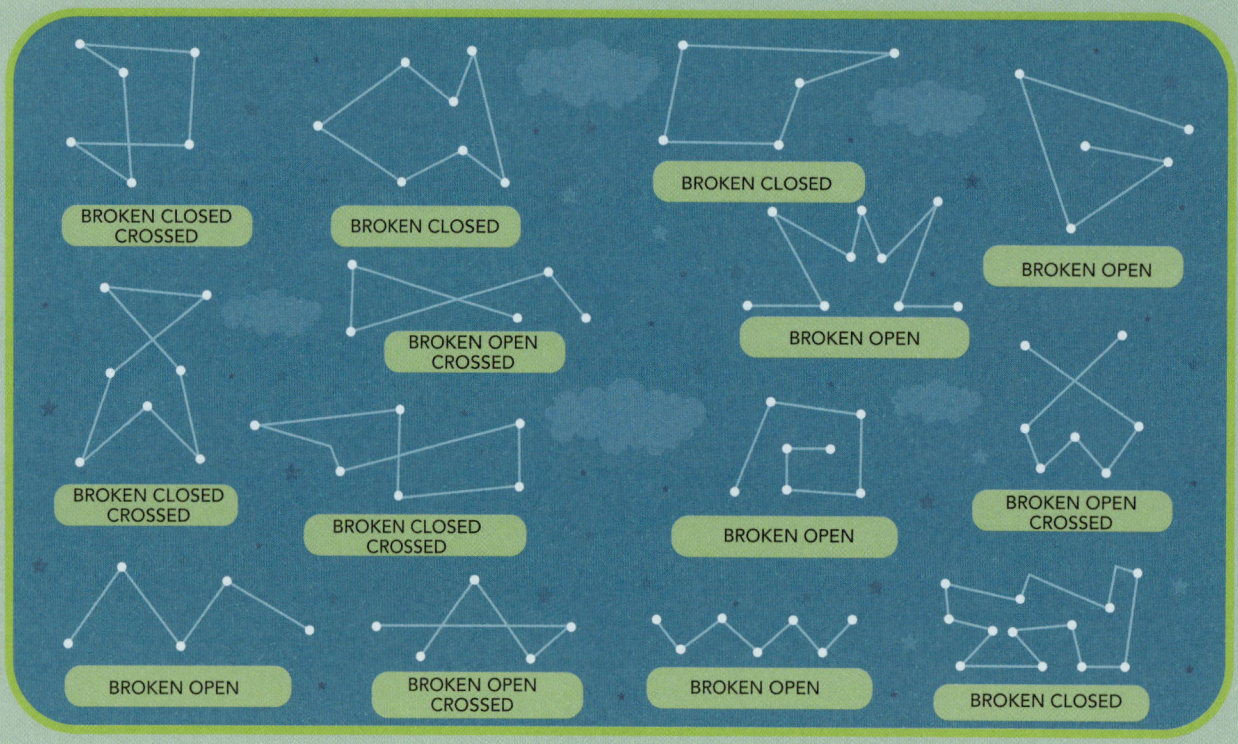

P. 9: ANGLES

P. 11: REGULAR AND IRREGULAR POLYGONS

PP. 12–13: SIDES AND ANGLES

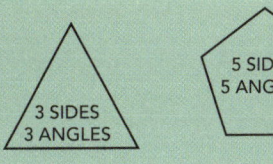
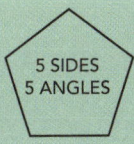
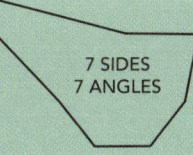

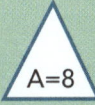
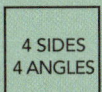

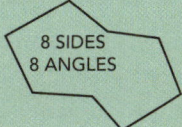
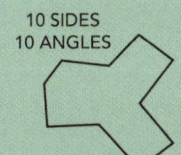
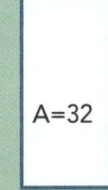
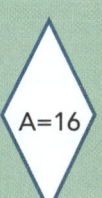

P. 15: AREAS

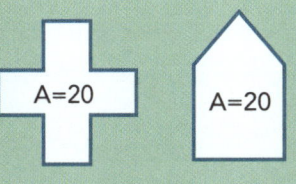
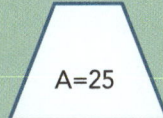
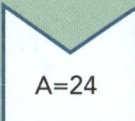
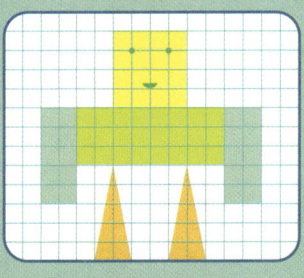

SIRIUS BOT AREA = 70

PP. 16–17: THE GALAXIES OF LABYRINTHS

P. 19: EULER'S THEOREM

TETRAHEDRON
FACES=4 EDGES=6 VERTICES=4
4 − 6 + 4 = 2

OCTAHEDRON
FACES=8 EDGES=12 VERTICES=6
8 − 12 + 6 = 2

DODECAHEDRON
FACES=12 EDGES=30 VERTICES=20
12 − 30 + 20 = 2

ICOSAHEDRON
FACES=20 EDGES=30 VERTICES=12
20 − 30 + 12 = 2

P. 26: HOW MANY SQUARES CAN YOU SEE?

1 = 40 SQUARES
2 = 30 SQUARES
3 = 45 SQUARES
4 = 28 SQUARES

P. 27: HOW MANY TRIANGLES CAN YOU SEE?

5 = 20 TRIANGLES
6 = 27 TRIANGLES
7 = 42 TRIANGLES
8 = 24 TRIANGLES

PP. 28–29: HOW MANY CAN YOU SEE?

P. 31: THE PLANET-ELEVATING MACHINE

PLANETS A AND C ARE RAISED.

P. 33: TANGRAM COMETS

PP. 34–35: ASTROTAXI DISTANCES

- HOW MANY UNITS CORRESPOND TO THE MINIMUM DISTANCE BETWEEN POINTS C AND D? **16**
- THE **BLUE** ROUTE IS THE SHORTEST
- **E-F:** MINIMUM DISTANCE **14**
- **G-H:** MINIMUM DISTANCE **10**

PP. 46–47: STELLAR MAPS

P. 51: THE WORLD OF CROTON

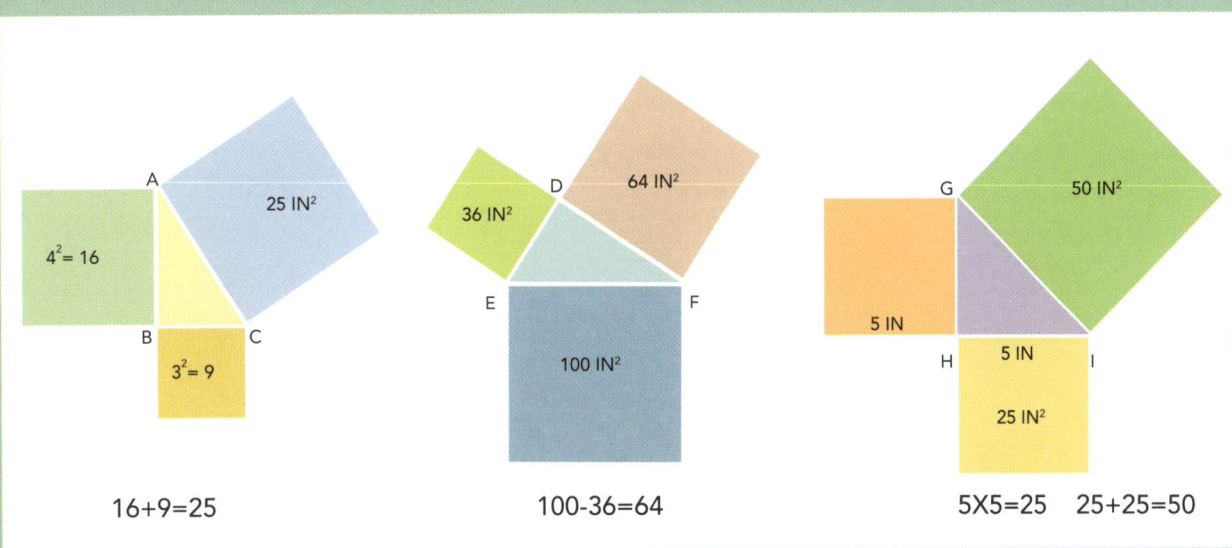

16+9=25   100−36=64   5X5=25   25+25=50

55

MATTIA CRIVELLINI

After graduating with a degree in information technology from the University of Bologna, Mattia went on to study cognitive sciences at Indiana University in Bloomington, Indiana. Since 2011, he has been the manager of Fosforo, the science festival of Senigallia. With the cultural organization NEXT, he organizes and plans events, shows, and conferences that showcase and promote science.

VALERIA BARATTINI

Valeria obtained a post-graduate degree in economics and management of the arts and cultural activities from the Ca' Foscari University of Venice, as well as a master's degree in standards for museum education from the Roma Tre University of Rome. She works in the fields of didactics and cultural planning. Since 2015, she has been collaborating with Fosforo, planning events and activities to promote science.

AGNESE BARUZZI

Agnese obtained a degree in graphic planning from ISIA (Superior Institute for the Arts Industries) in Urbino, Italy. Since 2001, she has been working as an illustrator and author. She has published numerous books for teenagers in Italy and abroad, collaborating with schools and libraries. In the last few years, she has enjoyed illustrating books for White Star Kids.

White Star Kids® is a registered trademark property of White Star s.r.l.

© 2020 White Star s.r.l.
Piazzale Luigi Cadorna, 6
20123 Milan, Italy
www.whitestar.it

Translation: Translation: TperTradurre srl, Rome
Editing: Michele Suchomel-Casey

All rights reserved. No part of this publication may be reproduced, stored in a retrieval system or transmitted in any form or by any means, electronic, mechanical, photocopying, recording or otherwise, without written permission from the publisher.

ISBN 978-88-544-1634-5
1 2 3 4 5 6   24 23 22 21 20

Printed in Poland

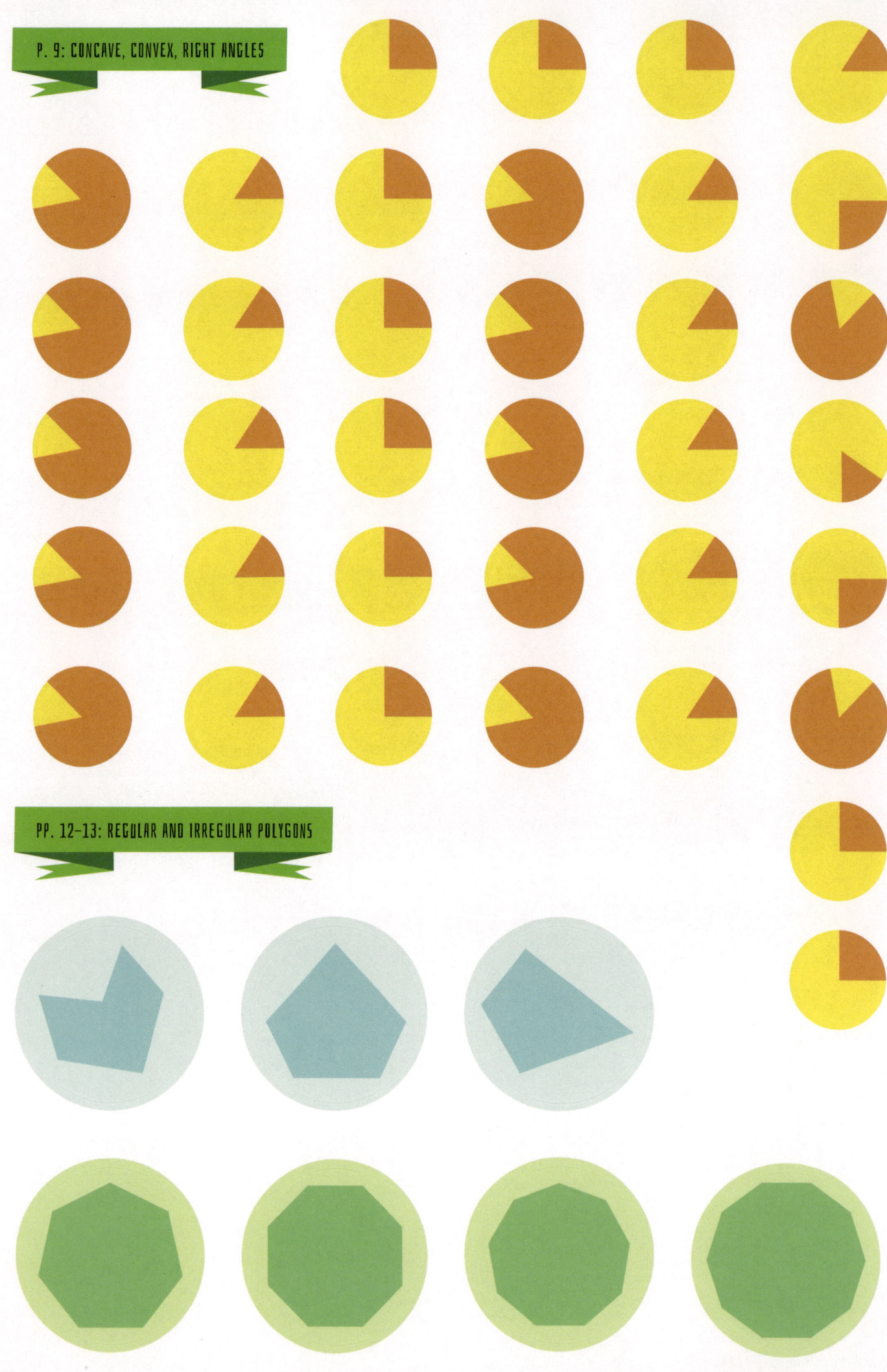

P. 33: THE TANGRAM AND THE COMETS

PP. 38-39: SYMMETRY AND ASTEROIDS

PP. 38-39: SYMMETRY AND ASTEROIDS

PP. 40–41: ROTATION AND TRANSLATION

P. 43: MOEBIUS STRIPS

P. 49: WOCH, THE MONOCLIMATE PLANET